A TREATISE
of CONVERSING
in HEAVEN and
WALKING with
GOD

Register This New Book

Benefits of Registering*

- ✓ FREE **replacements** of lost or damaged books
- ✓ FREE **audiobook** – *Pilgrim's Progress*, audiobook edition
- ✓ FREE information about new titles and other **freebies**

www.anekopress.com/new-book-registration

*See our website for requirements and limitations.

A TREATISE of CONVERSING in HEAVEN and WALKING with GOD

For our conversation is in heaven.
– PHILIPPIANS 3:20

JEREMIAH BURROUGHS

A Treatise of Conversing in Heaven and Walking with God
© 2025 by Aneko Press
All rights reserved. First edition 1652.
Revisions copyright 2025.

Please do not reproduce, store in a retrieval system, or transmit in any form or by any means – electronic, mechanical, photocopying, recording, or otherwise, without written permission from the publisher.

Scripture quotations are from The Authorized (King James) Version. Rights in the Authorized Version in the United Kingdom are vested in the Crown. Reproduced by permission of the Crown's patentee, Cambridge University Press.

Cover Designer: J. Martin, Jonathan Lewis
Cover Image: Name of Artist/Shutterstock, or Adobe Firefly
Editor: C. Miskimen

Aneko Press
www.anekopress.com
inquiries@anekopress.com
Aneko Press, Life Sentence Publishing, and our logos are trademarks of
Life Sentence Publishing, Inc.
203 E. Birch Street
P.O. Box 652
Abbotsford, WI 54405

RELIGION / Christian Living / Spiritual Growth
Paperback ISBN: 979-8-88936-555-6
eBook ISBN: 979-8-88936-556-3

10 9 8 7 6 5 4 3 2 1
Available where books are sold

Contents

To the Reader ix

A Heavenly Conversation

1. Learning from Godly Men 1
2. When Godly Examples Differ 7
3. Why Following the Example of the Wicked and Ignoring the Godly Leads to Ruin 9
4. The Saints' True Home Is Heaven – and How That Affects Their Life on Earth 13
5. What It Means to Be a Citizen of Heaven 15
6. How to Live as a Citizen of Heaven 19
7. Trading for Heaven: How the Saints Invest in Eternity 29
8. Seven Marks of a Life Anchored in Heaven 35
9. Why the Saints' Hearts Are Set on Heaven 41
10. A Warning to Those Living as Citizens of Hell 49
11. A Warning to Hypocrites Who Claim Heaven but Live for Earth 51
12. Why We Should Not Complain Against the Narrow Way of God 53
13. When Godly People Fall Short in Living a Heavenly Life 55
14. A Heavenly Life Is a Powerful Witness 59

15. A Heavenly Life Keeps Growing 63
16. A Heavenly Life Brings Glory to God 65
17. A Heavenly Life Brings Honor to the Saints..............................67
18. A Heavenly Life Makes Suffering Easier 69
19. A Heavenly Life Brings Joy 71
20. A Heavenly Life Is Secure 73
21. A Heavenly Life Opens Wide the Gates of Glory 75
22. How to Grow in a Heavenly Life..77

Walking With God

1. Opening the Text...89
2. The Excellence of a Christian Life: Walking with God 93
3. How the Soul Is Brought to Walk with God 97
4. What It Means to Walk with God 103
5. Twelve Blessings of Walking with God 117
6. Exhortations to Walk with God 129
7. Marks of a True Walk with God 137
8. Twelve Rules for Walking with God 151
9. When God Seems to Hide His Face: An Objection Answered.167
About the Author...173
Also by Jeremiah Burroughs 176

To the Reader

It was the saying of a servant of Christ, every day a Christian spends on earth, is a day lost in heaven. Certainly, he meant it of the place, not the company. For what makes heaven, but union and communion with God in Jesus Christ? Now this is attainable in this life. What hinders a Christian from living in heaven while he lives on earth? Truly our fellowship is with the Father, and with his Son Jesus Christ, 1 John 1:3. And our conversation is in heaven (another apostle says), Philippians 3:20. *I have been crucified with Christ; and it is no longer I who live, but Christ lives in me; and the life which I now live in the flesh I live by faith in the Son of God* (Galatians 2:20). These were men on earth, subject to such infirmities as these are, yet lived in heaven. There are those living now in this declining, deliberate and unprovoked, Christdenying age, a generation upon earth whose lives and graces, though hidden under a mean outside under many reproaches and infirmities, shine inwardly with the glory of Christ upon them. Even though they be in the world, they follow the Lord with a Spirit differing from the spirit of the world. Among these hidden ones of the Lord, this blessed man (the preacher of these sermons, of whom the world was not worthy) was such a one, who while he was upon earth, lived in heaven. As you may easily perceive, the end and scope of these sermons is to wind up your heart to a similar frame and posture. That is namely to take it off from perishing vanities and to set it upon that which is the real and durable substance.

We see upon what weak shoulders the fair neck of all worldly pomp and glory now stands. We see, too, how the Lord is winding up and putting an end to the glories of the kingdoms of men who have not contributed their strength and power to the advancing, but contrariwise, to the pulling down and eclipsing of the glory of the kingdom of Jesus Christ. Besides what the world tells us, never has any age by the works of providence, had more examples laid before them of the worlds vanity than in our days. Therefore our hearts should rid themselves of all things that cannot stretch themselves to eternity. The apostle's reason is full of weight: it remains (he said) that both they that have wives, be as though they had none, and they that weep, as though they wept not, and they that rejoice, as though they rejoiced not, and they that buy, as though they possessed not, and they that use the world, as not abusing it. He puts forth this exhortation using this argument: the time is short, or as the word is, the remainder of our season is now folding up as a sail or a curtain into a narrow room.

Time is short, life shorter, and the end of all things is at hand. We have greater things to tend to, and to set our hearts upon. The divinity of this holy man's spirit was greatly evident in this, that having much of the comfort that earth could afford him, he still looked upon all creatures contentment's with the eyes of a stranger. This was done to raise his soul up to a more holy, humble, serviceable, selfdenying walk with God.

For him that enjoys little or nothing in the world, it is easy for him to speak much of the world's vanity and emptiness because his heart was never taken with the sweetness the world offers. When surrounded with the confluence of creaturecomforts, it is not as hard then, by a divine spirit, to tread upon the neck of these things, be caught up into the third heaven, and there experience bathing, solacing and satisfying of itself with the sweet and higher enjoyments, with the more savory and cordial apprehensions from Jesus Christ. This is somewhat like him that is made partaker of the divine nature, and that lives above the world in the enjoyment of the world.

Now you have seen these sermons printed twice: once in the practice of this holy man, and now again in these papers which we present to you in this preaching style (though we confess things might have been more contracted). This preaching style because we find it more desired, more acceptable to his hearers, and if we are not wrong, it works more upon the affections, and is more profitable to a greater number of Christians. The Lord Jesus be with your spirit, and go along with these and all other his precious labors, to the furtherance of the joy of your faith, building you up in the inner man, and directing you in the way to your eternal rest.

Thomas Goodwyn,
William Greenhil,
Sydrach Simpson,
Philip Nye,
William Bridge,
John Yates,
William Adderley,

A Heavenly Conversation

For our conversation is in heaven.
– Philippians 3:20

Chapter 1

Learning from Godly Men

For our conversation is in heaven.
– Philippians 3:20

Some read the word "for" here as though it meant "but": *But our conversation is in heaven* – our conversation, our way of life, is not the same as theirs. Certainly Paul intended to show a sharp contrast between the saints' ways and the ways of those who are enemies of the cross of Christ, who *mind earthly things. But our conversation is in heaven* (Philippians 3:18-19).

But notice the actual wording: *For our conversation is in heaven.* The word "for" points us back to verse 17. Verses 18 and 19 are really a parenthesis, so if you want to understand the apostle's meaning, you must connect verse 20 with verse 17: *Brethren, be followers together of me, and mark them which walk so as you have us for an ensample. . . . For our conversation is in heaven.*

Paul digressed for a moment. First, he urged his listeners, "Make us your example." Then, by way of warning, he describes others: Many walk otherwise and are enemies of the cross of

Christ – *Whose end is destruction, whose God is their belly, and whose glory is in their shame, who mind earthly things.* After this digression, he returns to his main point: *For our conversation is in heaven.*

It is as though he said, "Be careful not to follow those whose belly is their god, who mind earthly things – for their end is destruction. Rather, follow those whose conversation is in heaven – for their end is salvation." In other words: Follow us as examples, for our conversation is in heaven. Such men are guided by the Spirit of God, and the end of their way is good; therefore, it is safe to follow them.

In Proverbs 2:20, the wise man gives a similar reason to embrace wisdom: It will teach you to *walk in the way of good men, and keep the paths of the righteous.* We are to observe the way of good men and hold fast to the paths of the righteous.

That said, even the best men – even the holiest – are not themselves a sufficient rule for any action. If a man or woman does something, however good in itself, merely because another person has done it, the action will be sin to them. Even if the thing is good, if it is done only because others have done it, it will still be sin. Why? Because Christ's rule is this: *Whatsoever is not of faith is sin* (Romans 14:23). No mere example can be a sufficient ground for faith. Therefore, example alone is not a good rule.

We know that Satan can transform himself into an angel of light and, to promote evil, may put on a great show of holiness. Many shameless hypocrites have also, for a time, maintained an outwardly holy life. It follows, then, as a sure truth: The examples of men – no matter how holy they may seem – are not a sufficient rule.

Yet, with this caution in mind, the examples of holy men should carry weight with us – at least to this extent:

More than other examples.

The examples of godly men should carry more force with us than those of the most learned men. Knowledge alone does not prove holiness. One holy man, whose conversation is in heaven, should be more persuasive to us than the example of many scholars, for many who are learned are also corrupt, and some even act against their own consciences.

Their examples should also weigh more with us than the examples of the great and the wealthy – those who have goods laid up for many years. It is better to follow the example of those who appear to be holy, even if they are poor, rather than the richest or most influential in your town.

> The examples of holy men should outweigh the example of the multitude.

Likewise, the examples of holy men should outweigh the example of the multitude. Scripture warns us against following the multitudes: *Multitudes, multitudes in the valley of decision* (Joel 3:14). The crowd often walks the way of destruction.

And their examples should carry more weight than the example of those who are merely related to us. Children should value the example of godly men and women – even strangers – more highly than that of father, mother, uncle, aunt, or any other near relative if those relatives are not walking in holiness. Though the examples of holy men are not rules for our faith, they should still have more influence on us than the examples of any others.

Enough to remove prejudice.

While not a rule of faith, the example of the godly should be strong enough to remove prejudices stirred up by false accusations of men against the ways of God. Suppose people speak bitterly against a certain way of worship – charging it with falsehoods because it is not the established, national way of worship and because few follow it. In such cases, observe the lives of the people who do worship in that way. Are they not holy and blameless according to the gospel, the strictest Puritans? Even if we must not imitate them merely for their example's sake, their example should still powerfully influence us to soften our spirits, remove our prejudice, and silence false accusations.

Enough to stir inquiry.

Even though examples are not sufficient grounds for faith, the examples of upright, godly men are enough to move us to examine the ways they follow and test them by the Word of God. Because these people are such close friends of Jesus Christ, there is a strong probability that these ways are the paths of Zion and lead to the gate of heaven. Those who converse most with God are most likely to know His mind. One who is a familiar friend, who talks daily with God, is more likely to know His secrets and His will than a stranger. Of all people on earth, only the saints are no longer strangers to God. They talk with Him: they are people of His heart and His counsel; therefore, they are the ones most likely to have God's will revealed to them

Learning and natural wisdom cannot reveal God's mind as much as daily, humble conversation with God can. God loves to open His heart to His hidden ones, to make known His mind to them. Therefore, when we see godly men – whose conversation is in heaven – walking in certain ways, it should make us think that there is more good in those ways than we see right now. We must not instantly conclude that what they do is the mind of God and follow them for that reason alone, but we should carefully examine their ways in the light of Scripture.

Enough to restrain opposition.

We should be very slow to oppose the ways of godly men unless we have very clear scriptural ground to do so. If such grounds exist, then we may oppose them, as Paul opposed Peter and resisted him to his face because he was wrong. Even the holiest and most godly people can err. If, after examining their actions by the Word of God and by conscience, we find they do not align with God's will – not simply because others object to them, but because the actions do not line up with the mind of God – then we may speak or write against them. Not until then.

And if we do oppose, we must be certain in our consciences and sure of our scriptural grounds, so that we are not in danger of fighting against God when we oppose them. The example of holy, godly men is not absolute authority, but it is weighty enough that we should not resist it lightly. If we do disagree, let it be because God's Word clearly shows their way to be wrong.

Enough to prepare our hearts for truth.

When we examine the ways of God and heaven, we must approach with prepared hearts, ready to receive the truths He will reveal to us – even more so when we see that holy and godly men have embraced those truths before us. Gospel truths delivered to us through the hands of the servants of Jesus Christ are like *apples of gold in pictures of silver* (Proverbs 25:11), as beautiful as golden fruit in silver dishes.

Enough to confirm and strengthen us.

Once we have examined a way and found it to be according to the truth, then the example of godly men walking in it should confirm us in that truth. Their example should comfort and encourage us as we walk, because not only are we convinced of it through the study of the Word of God, but we also see other godly people finding communion with God in the same way. Seeing that others are convinced it is the way of God will strengthen us on our journey because it confirms for us that we are on the same road as the saints of God. It is a great joy when saints walk together in the same way, with their faces toward heaven.

Yet here in this world, there will always be differences among the godly, for here we are imperfect. Sometimes a weak Christian may know something that a stronger one does not. God may reveal certain things to those who are weak and hide them from others. Until New Jerusalem descends from heaven, the saints will not all be of one mind or walk fully in one way. Still, it should grieve godly men when they must part ways and walk in a different path than other godly men. And it should greatly comfort and encourage them whenever they can walk together in unity, pressing on side by side toward their eternal home in heaven.

Chapter 2

When Godly Examples Differ

If you ask, "What should we do when godly men give contrary examples – both of them holy men, whose conduct is heavenly, but some go one way and others, just as godly, go another?" What then, when both sides are led by men of evident holiness?

I reply to this with two things:

First, God uses this very situation to press us to a more careful examination of things. By it, He teaches that every Christian, however weak, must have a sure foundation for his faith and practice drawn from the Word of God. We must not be content in any matter of religion unless we can find for ourselves clear footing for it in Scripture.

In earlier times, Christians were greatly swayed by examples. A few eminent and godly leaders would carry all the well-affected in those places with them, and all who leaned toward godliness would be reluctant to walk in a way different from these men. Yet though their intentions were good (and God may accept their sincerity), they were not as grounded and established in the truth as God desires. But now the Lord seems to be dealing with His people differently. He calls even the weakest and lowest believer to search and know the truth for themselves. We hope it is time for God to fulfill His promise: *They shall be all taught of God* (John 6:45). When Christians come to understand the grounds of their beliefs and practices for themselves, their faith is much stronger, and they are more firmly established than they ever were before.

Second, when you see godly examples going in opposite directions, examine carefully which way has more earthly inducements. For whatever way has more worldly advantages to draw or bias the heart is the way that lies under the most suspicion. Even the most godly men are godly only in part, and while they may be upright in many things, they may also be tempted by worldly contentment. If such temptation presses more on one side than the other, be more cautious of that way. But this is not the main point, so we move on.

Chapter 3

Why Following the Example of the Wicked and Ignoring the Godly Leads to Ruin

If we are to follow the example of those whose conduct is heavenly, then it follows that we should rebuke those who imitate the example of the wicked and ungodly – whether because such men are great or learned or simply because there are many of them. Some will follow the example of anyone rather than the example of those whose lives are in heaven. You excuse yourself by saying, "Do not others do the same?"

But who are these others? Can you honestly say that those you imitate have their conversation in heaven? Will you do what they do? If you follow any example, you should be able to be clear in your conscience that these people live their lives above. Will you drink because they drink, swear because they swear, break the Sabbath because they do, and walk in profaneness because they walk in it? If so, know that you are following those whose conversation is not in heaven, but in hell.

Perhaps you live near neighbors whose conduct is blameless, even heavenly. Sometimes, your conscience testifies to their holiness, and you wish you might die the death of the righteous. Are there not some in your own family or in your street or town whose lives you admire, though at times you scorn, oppose, and speak against them? When you are sober-minded or afraid of death, would you not rather be as they are and die their death? Why then do you not follow their example instead of the example of those who live only to satisfy their vile and sinful lusts?

These examples of holy men will rise up in judgment against you another day. The Lord will say, "Did not these people live in your household and your neighborhood? Did you not see their holy and gracious lives? Yet you chose to follow the example of vile wretches instead of the example of My saints?" This will silence your mouths and aggravate your condemnation in the great Day of Account.

Some go even further – not only do they refuse to follow the godly, but they also rage against them. They do what they can to darken the brightness of their holy lives. If any slander or misreporting arises, they eagerly spread it, hoping to eclipse the holiness of the saints' lives so that they may stop their own consciences. If there was not something to darken the brilliance and beauty of the lives of the saints, these people's own hearts would condemn them for walking in such contrary ways. To quiet their consciences, they throw dirt on the righteous and are glad to hear bad reports about them. Their corrupt hearts are set against the holiness of the saints.

Finally, let those who profess religion take care to walk so that their example convicts and persuades others. If holy examples carry such power, then you who claim to follow Christ must labor to keep your lives fixed in heaven so that your example

> Let those who profess religion take care to walk so that their example convicts and persuades others.

may do more good in the place where you live. But if you profess religion while clinging to worldly ways, living scandalous and vile lives, you do immense harm. There is no greater mischief than for a man to profess Christ yet live wickedly – thereby giving the lie to his profession. But I have spoken about this elsewhere when I treated that Scripture: *Only let your conversation be as it becometh the gospel of Christ* (Philippians 1:27).

Chapter 4

The Saints' True Home Is Heaven – and How That Affects Their Life on Earth

Now, we proceed to the main doctrinal truths in this passage: *For our conversation is in heaven.* That is, our city life, our citizen-like behavior, our conduct as free citizens belongs to heaven.

From this we learn two things:

1. The saints are the citizens of heaven.
2. Their behavior and manner of life, even while they are in this world, is to be heavenly.

I will just speak briefly to the first point: The saints of God are truly citizens of heaven. They are all free denizens, fellow citizens of heaven. Ephesians 2:19 says: *Now therefore ye are no more strangers and foreigners, but fellowcitizens with the saints, and of the household of God.* God has gathered His saints into this heavenly city, the church. The church on earth is a kind of heaven, a type and foretaste of the everlasting heaven where the saints and angels will live together forever.

Hebrews 11:9-10 speaks of Abraham: *By faith, he sojourned in the land of promise, as in a strange country, dwelling in tabernacles with Isaac and Jacob, the heirs with him of the same promise: for he looked for a city which hath foundations, whose builder and maker is God.* All the cities of this world, in comparison, have no true foundations, for they are built by men – and often by wicked and ungodly men. Abraham was looking for a city built by God. The first city that we read of in Scripture was built by Cain. But Abraham sought the city of God, whose foundations are firm and whose builder is God Himself.

Abraham was looking for a city built by God.

Hebrews 12:22 says: *But ye are come unto mount Sion, and unto the city of the living God, the heavenly Jerusalem, and to an innumerable company of angels.* Here the saints are called citizens of the heavenly Jerusalem, which is here in the church. Yet since angels are also included as fellow citizens, this shows the reference is not only to the church on earth but also to the glory of heaven itself.

So, even now, the saints may be said to dwell in heaven because they belong to the church and because they are already enrolled as citizens of that eternal heaven in which they will live forever. Revelation 13 speaks of the beast blaspheming against God: *And he opened his mouth in blasphemy against God, to blaspheme his name, and his tabernacle, and them that dwell in heaven. And it was given unto him to make war with the saints, and to overcome them* (Revelation 13:6-7). Now these were not in heaven. They were still on earth in their bodies, yet Scripture says they *dwell in heaven*, for their true citizenship is there. As members of the church, they are free denizens of the heaven, too, in which they will live later in a more glorious way. In this sense, they are already heavenly men and women, citizens of that eternal city. We will see this truth later when we discuss their conversation being in heaven.

Chapter 5

What It Means to Be a Citizen of Heaven

Now the saints are citizens of heaven, and this may be shown in many ways.

Their names are recorded there. Luke 10:20 says: *Rejoice, because your names are written in heaven.* In heaven is the Book of Life, where the names of all the saints are written. Paul told the Philippians to help his fellow laborers, *whose names are in the book of life* (Philippians 4:3).

They are citizens of heaven because Christ, their Head, has already gone before them to take possession on their behalf. As a person is still considered a citizen of a place, even while he is traveling in another country, because his name is enrolled there and has his rights there – so the saints are citizens of heaven. Their names are written there, and Christ their Head has gone before in their names to take possession for them and to provide everything they need (John 14).

When they come to believe, they take up their freedom as citizens. Their names were written in heaven from all eternity, Christ secured their inheritance at His ascension, but when they come to belief themselves, they claim their freedom in the heavenly city. Just as those who are serving for their freedom may have to wait a long time to be free and those who are born free may not immediately claim their privileges but do so at a certain time, so the saints in believing take up their liberty as free citizens of heaven.

They are no longer slaves. They have been delivered from bondage and made free. By nature, they were slaves of sin, Satan, and the Law; but when they believe and are enfranchised into the heavenly city, they are delivered from all bondage and made free citizens. As slaves who are admitted into a free city come to share in the same rights and freedoms that others have, so the saints are freed from the bondage of sin and given the freedom of the city of heaven.

All the saints share in the common stock, the treasury, and the riches of heaven. Whatever privileges belong to the charter of heaven, the saints have right and title to them all. As in great cities there is a common treasury that is for public occasions and every citizen has some interest in it, so all believers have a right to every privilege of belonging to heaven and an interest in all its riches.

Though their bodies are not yet in the highest heaven, the saints, as citizens of heaven, already enjoy the same confirmation of happiness as the angels and those blessed souls who are resident in heaven have. The angels and the souls in Abraham's bosom are confirmed in a happy state so that they cannot be made miserable – and so is every believer. Though he lives in this world, because he is a citizen of heaven, he is established in a happy state, and all the powers in hell and in the world can never make this soul miserable. This is a mighty privilege of being a citizen of heaven. He is more privileged than Adam in Paradise, for he was not confirmed and established when he was made in the state of innocence; he could still fall. But every believer is confirmed and established forever, as the angels in heaven are.

They have the privilege of free trade with heaven. In earthly cities, freemen may trade freely, while foreigners must pay duties and heavy charges. So the saints have the privilege of free access and trade with heaven for anything that concerns them. They have free relations with heaven that others do not have.

They enjoy communion with the angels of heaven. Since they are fellow citizens of the same heavenly city, there is communion and interaction between the saints here and the angels. We are come to *the heavenly Jerusalem, and to an innumerable company of angels* (Hebrews 12:22). There is a great deal of contact between the saints and angels here on earth; the angels look on the saints as their fellow citizens and are ministering spirits for the good of the elect. Because they see them as fellow citizens, they do many services for the people of the church here in this world.

As citizens of heaven, they have the protection of heaven. Citizens have the protection of the laws of their city and have the power of their city to defend them. Because Paul was a citizen of Rome, it was dangerous to meddle with him: *As they bound him with thongs, Paul said unto the centurion that stood by, Is it lawful for you to scourge a man that is a Roman, and uncondemned?* (Acts 22:25). He was saying, "Be careful. I am a free citizen of Rome." When the centurion heard that, he told the chief captain to be careful what he did. The prisoner is a Roman with the protections of that city.

> Those who harm the saints ought to beware, for the saints are citizens of heaven

The saints are not citizens of Rome but of the heavenly Jerusalem. Those who harm the saints ought to beware, for the saints are citizens of heaven, protected by the King of heaven – who sits and laughs at the enemies of the church. The angels themselves are their guards and protectors.

They are taught by the Holy Spirit to have good and holy manners that are suitable for heaven. Being citizens of such an extraordinary city, the people of God should walk in a way becoming of such a privilege. It is shameful for citizens to live rudely, as untrained country folk might. But God has given His people the Spirit to instruct them in holy conduct worthy of heaven.

Therefore, prize your great privilege. It cost Jesus Christ His life to purchase this enfranchisement and liberty for you. In that story in Acts of Paul's Roman citizenship, when the captain heard that Paul was a Roman, he said to Paul, *Tell me, art thou a Roman? He said, Yea. And the chief captain answered, With a great sum obtained I this freedom. And Paul said, But I was free born* (Acts 22:27-28). Earthly citizenship often came at great cost, and the freedom of Rome was purchased with large sums of money. But the freedom of heaven was purchased by the blood of Christ, a price far above all the world.

This city we are speaking of has privileges beyond any in this world. And no man or woman can say as Paul that they were born free. Those with the freedom of heaven have it because Jesus purchased it with His blood that was worth more than all the world. *If the Son therefore shall make you free, ye shall be free indeed* (John 8:36).

Prize this citizenship as a great privilege. While you live here in this world, value this privilege as the greatest mercy. It is true you have no habitation here in the wilderness of this world, but God has enrolled you as a free citizen of heaven, your eternal home.

Chapter 6

How to Live as a Citizen of Heaven

But now, our conversation, our way of life, ought to match this reality. And here we come to the apostle's main point: *Our conversation is in heaven.*

The lives of the saints should reflect the reality that they are free citizens of heaven. Though they live in this world, their conversation is in heaven. *But the saints of the most High shall take the kingdom, and possess the kingdom for ever* (Daniel 7:18). What is meant here is that the saints are not only saints of the Most High God but also saints of the high places. Some have even translated it that way because of their interest in heaven and because their lives are suited for it.

Ephesians 2:6 says: *And hath raised us up together, and made us sit together in heavenly places in Christ Jesus.* The saints are set in heavenly places and given heavenly dignities, privileges, and prerogatives. Though their bodies are on earth, their souls are in heavenly places. They are the saints of God and are set in high places.

What is this conversation that is in heaven?

The aim of the saints is heavenly. They look on themselves as pilgrims and strangers in this world and are seeking a better country. Heaven is their home, what they are looking at, where they place their treasures, and the reason for everything they do. If they eat, if they drink, if they work, it is with an eye on heaven.

The philosopher Anaxagoras was asked why he lived. He replied that he was born to contemplate the heavens. Having some understanding of the motions of the heavens, he took such great delight in it that he called it the reason he was born. So the saints look to heaven as the aim of their lives. Paul said: *We look not at the things which are seen, but at the things which are not seen* (2 Corinthians 4:18). Their conversation is in heaven because that is where they look for everything.

Their principles are heavenly. Heavenly actions must come from heavenly principles.

What are heavenly principles?

One heavenly principle that the saints are guided by is that *God is all in all.* In heaven, they look to God to be all in all for them. So, here, the saints, in what they do, in what they are, and in what they enjoy, act on this principle. God is all in all. No matter what I see in the creature, it is God that is all in all, so I will base my actions on this principle.

That *God, the infinite First-being, is infinitely worthy of all love* is a heavenly principle. The saints in heaven look on the infinite excellence and glory of God. They look on Him as the First-Being of all things, who has all excellencies, and is gloried enough to satisfy all creatures forever. They look on Him as infinitely worthy of all love and service. If I look to things of the world to increase my credit, wealth, or comfort, I am acting on earthly principles. But when my heart is so set on God that it looks on Him as infinitely excellent and worthy of all love, service, fear, honor, and worship – that no matter what becomes of the creature, God is worthy of all because of the infinite excellencies in Himself – then I am acting on a heavenly principle. Those whose conversation is in heaven are not acting on the same low principles as the men of the world are but on heavenly principles.

Their communion is in heaven. Though they live here in the world, they have communion with the God of heaven that is above during the whole course of their lives. There are many excellent words about our communion with God in 1 John 1: *That which we have seen and heard declare we unto you, that ye also may have fellowship with us: and truly our fellowship is with the Father, and with his Son Jesus Christ* (1 John 1:3). In another Scripture we read of the communion of the Holy Spirit (2 Corinthians 13:14).

Now what makes heaven but God? Where the king is, there is the court; where God is, there is heaven, let God be where He will. There is some controversy among some about where the saints will be after the resurrection – some think it will be still here but with all the glory that the Scripture speaks of. It does not matter where it is as long as it is where God is. Those who have communion with God are in heaven, and their conversation is in heaven.

The life of a Christian is communion with God. On earth we have communion with created things. The human faculties – our senses, appetites, and desires – were made to have delight when they encounter a suitable object. For many, that is all life is – communion with the creature. For example, a drunkard has a kind of communion with crude company and

> Those whose conversation is in heaven are not acting on the same low principles as the men of the world.

with alcohol to please his senses for a while. That is all the communion he has. What a difference there is between one whose only life is to please his senses with food and drink and one who has communion with the Father, Son, and Holy Spirit! The communion of believers with God is not imaginary but a real fellowship with the triune God.

By communion with God we mean this: It is the soul acting upon God and the soul receiving into itself the influence of God's goodness, mercy, and love. It is when the soul moves toward God and God moves upon the soul again. As when friends have communion with one another, each one acts for the comfort of the other; there is a mutual embracing and opening of hearts, each one seeking to satisfy the spirit of the other. So communion with God is this mutual working: the soul on God and God on the soul. The saints see the face of God, and God delights in the face of the saints. They pour out their hearts to God, and God pours out His heart to them.

This cannot be explained to strangers. A stranger cannot meddle with this joy. It is a mystery, a riddle to the carnal world. Consider this: the communion you have with your crude company – sitting, eating, drinking, playing, and telling stories all day long – you think that is a fine life. But the communion of the saints is raised far higher. Their comfort is not in such low, poor things as yours but in God the Father, Son, and Holy Spirit, in an infinitely higher way. In that respect, their conversation is said to be in heaven.

Especially when they are with God in His ordinances, they cannot be content unless they have communion with God there. It is not enough for them to call upon the name of God, to kneel, and to speak some humble, broken-hearted words. Instead, they cry, "What communion have I with God, Jesus Christ, and the Holy Spirit in my duties at this time? I come to the Word and other ordinances, but what communion do

I have with God in them? I cannot be satisfied except I taste and see how good the Lord is. I cannot go about my business with a cheerful heart unless I hear something from heaven this morning!" All the comfort of their lives depends on having communion with the Father, Son, and Holy Spirit.

Their conversation may be said to be in heaven because they live according to the laws of heaven. They do not live here by the laws and desires of men, but they look for their direction from heaven. What rule is there from heaven to guide me? they ask. There must be some word from the God of heaven to order and guide them in their ways or else they would not know how to obey them. It is true that while they live in the cities of the world, they must obey the laws of men, but only as those laws agree with the higher laws of heaven. The Christian submits first to the statute laws of Jesus Christ, the great Lawgiver.

Because the law of heaven commands them to obey just laws on earth, they do so. But their first concern before they do anything is: Does the law of heaven allow this? Do I have any word from Jesus Christ to guide me in such a way? I dare not do otherwise than according to the will and scepter of Christ – they must be my rule in everything I do. Once their lusts and worldly ends ruled them, but now they are ruled by the laws of heaven.

Their conversations are in heaven because they are guided by the laws of heaven. Their aim is heaven, their principles are heavenly, their communion is with the God of heaven – and they live according to the laws of heaven.

Their thoughts and hearts are set on heaven. It is said: *The soul is where it loves rather than where it lives.* Where the heart is, there the soul is also, and there the man may be said to be. The saints have their hearts in heaven; their thoughts and meditations are in heaven. David said, *When I awake, I am still with thee* (Psalm 139:18). And how sweet are the thoughts of heaven to the saints!

While you are muddling along in the world and plodding for yourself in the things of this world, God could come to you and say, "Where are you?" as He said to Adam. Even when you are at prayer or listening to the preaching of the Word, your thoughts are "wool gathering," wandering and distracted from God. But the person whose conversation is in heaven keeps his thoughts and meditations there continually, thinking on the glorious things that are laid up in heaven.

I remember reading a story about that holy man, Mr. Ward. In the middle of dinner, he fell into deep thought. Asked what he was pondering, he suddenly cried out, "Forever, forever, forever!" and for nearly a quarter of an hour could not be stilled. That is the thought of men and women whose hearts are in heaven. They are thinking of eternity: O eternity! To be forever in heaven with Christ and God! O the crown of glory that is there! When will that blessed day come when I will enjoy those good things that are there? His thoughts will be there, he is longing to be there, and his love, desires, and affections will be working there.

By contrast, we read of the people of Israel that *their hearts turned back again into Egypt* (Acts 7:39). Their bodies did not return, but their hearts were there. Their hearts desired the food and the comforts of Egypt. So also, many today hear the Word, yet their hearts are in their shops or bound up in covetousness. But it is different with the saints: Though they live here in this world, their hearts are in heaven.

It was said of Queen Mary that if she were cut open, Calais would be found in her heart. So it is with the saints whose conversations are in heaven. If they were cut open, you would find heaven in their hearts. I am not speaking of everyone who professes Christ, for Paul, when he spoke of the resurrection, said there are celestial bodies and terrestrial bodies. So I say there are celestial professors and terrestrial professors. Those whose conversations are in heaven, who walk with God, and live here the lives of heaven on earth, have heaven in their hearts. But open up the hearts of many and you would find nothing but the earth, filth, and vanity. If God were to open your heart right now and expose it to the whole world, what filth would be found there?

But those whom this text is describing would be ready for God to open their hearts. *Search me, O God, and know my heart* (Psalm 139:23). I will ask you in the name of God to answer honestly: What do you think would be found in your hearts if they were opened now? Perhaps your conscience would have to say, O Lord! If my heart would be ripped open now, there would be ugly and abominable filth there. I have not had my conversation in heaven. My heart has been sinking down to low and base things.

But it would be comforting to some. I hope there are many of you who could say, "Lord, if my heart were revealed, I hope the world would see that heaven is stamped on my heart."

We say the weather is sad when we cannot see the heavens for many days, and a house is in a bad location if it is in such a narrow city lane that people cannot see the sky unless they go out to the fields. Certainly, it is sad for a gracious heart when even one day passes without sight of heaven, without meditations of heaven, without communion there. Christians whose conversations are in heaven should never want to stay in a place where they cannot see the beams of the Sun.

It is a comforting thing to see the light. It is comforting for someone who lives in a dark house to walk out in the open air and look at the heavens. O my brothers and sisters! Every one of our souls dwells in a dark house, for our bodies are to our souls like a dark and low cellar. But the Lord gives us liberty to go abroad and converse with the things of heaven that He has revealed in His Word and in His ordinances. As people who work long hours in dark rooms find it refreshing and delightful to walk out in the fresh and open air on their days off, so too, a busy Christian, burdened with worldly business, rejoices when the Lord's Day comes. Now he may enjoy and commune with God more than before. He thinks on the ways he can have more of heaven. The Sabbaths are the joy of his soul, his delight. He longs for the Sabbath, and he thirsts after the ordinances, for his heart is truly in them. He finds there is more of heaven in them than in other things, and in this, he proves that his conversation is in heaven.

Moses never came to Canaan, yet God carried him up to Mount Nebo and let him see the promised land. Heavenly meditation is our Mount Nebo from which the heart is able to see heaven and the glorious things there. The Scripture says of Lucifer that he had his nest among the stars – but the saint's dwelling is above the stars, in the highest heavens. The wicked draw near outwardly to God while their hearts are far away in their shops or on their ships. But the saints, whose bodies seem to be far from God, keep their hearts in heaven itself.

A heavenly conversation is seen when, in the course of life, believers delight in the same things that are done in heaven. They make their happiness the same happiness that is in heaven and make their exercise to be the same exercise that is in heaven. For example, what is done in heaven? There, the blessed behold the face of God: *Blessed are the pure in heart: for they shall see God* (Matthew 5:8). And the angels *always behold the face* of God (Matthew 18:10). So, the saints may be said to have their conversations in heaven because their exercise here while they live is beholding the face of God, in standing before God and seeing His face. The greatest delight and contentment of their souls is that they can see God.

What else is done in heaven? The work of heaven is praising and blessing God. The saints and angels continually bless, magnify, and praise the name of the God whom they see to be so infinitely worthy of all praise and honor. A man's conversation is in heaven when he does the same things, when he joins with angels and saints in the same work of blessing, magnifying, and praising God.

What else? Heaven is a place of perpetual Sabbath. Our conversations are in heaven when we delight in God's Sabbath and when we keep a spiritual and constant Sabbath – resting from sin and being employed in holy things, even when occupied with earthly matters.

Our conversation is heavenly when engaged in earthly employments, we still use earthly things in a heavenly matter. It is not the place God looks at so much but the spirit in which His people live and what they do. Though we must use earthly things while we live on the earth, when we use them in a heavenly manner, then our conversation may be in heaven.

This happens, first, when we use earthly things only as a passage to God. We make use of them, but we do not rest in them. They are not our portion but our pathway to God. A carnal heart clings to the things of the world and mingles with the earth, but a spiritual, heavenly heart makes earthly things a conduit that carries it upward to heaven. For now, we carry with us the flesh and cannot be without earthly provisions; but they are vehicles that lift our thoughts to spiritual and heavenly things.

And again it happens when we use earthly things as occasions to meditate on heavenly ones. Every enjoyment in this life should raise our thoughts toward heaven and the life to come. If we see light, we think of the glorious light of heaven and the inheritance of the saints in light. If we taste sweetness in any earthly thing, we say, "If this is sweet, how much more is heaven and God Himself who is the fountain of all good things!" To use earthly things for heavenly contemplation is a heavenly conversation.

Our conversation is heavenly when the fellowship of the saints is heavenly. When they meet together, they see themselves as citizens of heaven and speak as is fitting of a citizen of that country. Englishmen abroad in foreign lands will meet and talk together in the language of their homeland about their country, their friends, and the bonds between them and say, "It feels like being in England again." So it should be with the saints. Their meetings should feel like being already in heaven. They do not meet to quarrel but to speak of their country and share news from above.

When Englishmen meet in a foreign country, the first thing they ask is for news from home. When the saints meet together, if they are of a heavenly conversation, they will be talking of heaven before they leave. Being earthly creatures, they may refresh themselves with some things of the earth, but they will talk of heaven before they part. That is the communion of the saints whose conversation is heavenly.

The last part of heavenly conversation is that the chief trade of the saints while they are on earth is for heaven. Their bodies are not there, but their business is there. This even seems to be noted in the very word of the text; their merchandise and their trading is in heaven.

The saints who have more heavenly conversations do not trade for trifles as other men do, but they trade for great things, for high things. Paul wrote: *If ye then be risen with Christ, seek those things which are above, where Christ sitteth on the right hand of God. Set your affections on things above, not on things on the earth* (Colossians 3:1-2). They seek the things of God. Their hearts are set on heavenly treasure, their commerce is with God, and they are trading for the pearl of great price.

Chapter 7

Trading for Heaven: How the Saints Invest in Eternity

In the saints' trading for heaven, several things must be considered.

First, every trade requires skill in the goods being handled. So it is with the saints: **They have skill in heavenly things**. Many poor Christians may have little knowledge in the affairs of the world. If you speak to them of earthly matters, they would understand very little. But speak to them about heaven, and it soon appears that they are skilled in heavenly commodities. This is a skill from God; they are wise merchants in spiritual things.

Every tradesman must also have stock to trade with. So too, the saints have a stock for their heavenly trade: **They have grace in their hearts**. Grace in the heart is the stock of a Christian's trade. A father who leaves his children no land but gives them a trade and stock to begin with has not left them poor. Though the saints have little in this world, they have both skill in heavenly commodities and a good stock. They have a stock of grace that will never be lost. They may not always receive the incomes they desire, but they will never lose their stock, their portion. And it should be their chief concern to improve that stock for heaven. Indeed, they may be said to have their conversation in heaven when they lay out and employ all their stock upon heavenly commodities.

In trading, one must take advantage of the market. Great bargains may sometimes be had that cannot be had at another time. So too, **the Christian's trade for heaven lies in observing the advantages God gives for heavenly things**. Those who have their conversations in heaven are very wise and understanding in this way: They are able to discern their times and seasons. But others, who lack skill in heavenly matters, do not know their opportunities, so they neglect their market. It may be on their sickbed or at the point of death that they begin to think of heaven. It is then that they long to know if their souls will go to heaven when they leave their bodies. But they were unskilled in heavenly commodities; they did not know their time. They should have had their conversation in heaven during the course of their lives and taken advantage of the opportunities God gave them for trading there.

Oh, that we were all wise in this way! For there is not one of us that God has not, at one time or another, given advantages for heaven – if only we had taken them. Think back on your own lives and your conscience will tell you that you had fair advantages for heaven. There were seasons when the Spirit of God stirred in you and darted truths into your soul. Holy motions were flowing in your heart. How happy you would have been if you had taken those opportunities for heaven! You would have even been in heaven already.

Now those who do converse with heaven watch for those opportunities. They do not come just to casually hear the Word, but they watch for the moment that God softens their spirits and enlivens their souls. They follow hard after those advantages. Thus they trade for heaven and grow rich in heavenly commodities.

Trade between countries involves a great deal of interaction between those countries. A man who trades with a certain town or country communicates often with those who live there. So in a Christian who is trading for heaven, **there is a considerable amount of interaction between heaven and his soul**. Every day he sends up something to heaven, and every day he receives something from heaven back to his soul.

Examine yourselves. What communication is there between heaven and you? For many of you, it is as if there were no heaven at all. Just as men who never trade to the Indies live as if no such place existed, so many, even some in the heart of the church, live as if there is no heaven. There is very little interaction between heaven and them. But the true trader for heaven has much contact there.

A man who trades for great matters keeps the chief of his stock in the place where he trades. Though he himself may not be present there, the main part of his estate is there. If a man is a Spanish merchant, his riches are chiefly in Spain; if a Turkish merchant, they lie more in Turkey than here. So it is with one who trades for heaven: **The greater part of his estate lies in heaven**. He accounts his true riches to be there. Indeed, he has something here in this world to live on for a while, but his real treasure is in heaven, and he looks there for his wealth.

> What communication is there between heaven and you?

A tradesman is willing to part with something where he lives to gain an advantage in the place where he trades. So it is with the saints who trade for heaven. **They are willing to part with much here so that they might receive abundantly in heaven.** They are willing and content to part with anything here in this world so that they may receive it when they come home.

A merchant abroad, preparing to return to his own country, will willingly spend all his money where he is to receive commodities in his trade in the country to which he belongs. In the same way, the saints are willing to live poorly and moderately here so that they might have riches laid up in their mansion in glory. But the carnal heart that does not know the certainty nor excellency of the commodities of heavenly things is unwilling to part with anything. They think to themselves, "We are sure of what we have here. We do not understand all that talk of heaven. We do not know what it is – it might all be imaginary. So we will keep all that we have because we are sure of that." They cling to the world and will not trade for heaven. Those who do trade for heaven are willing to part with anything here to gain riches there.

Those who trade for great matters must wait and trust. Merchants trading by retail take in pence and shillings daily, but wholesale merchants often receive little or nothing at the time of sale – they must wait for their great returns. So it is with those who trade for heaven. **They live by trust.** Faith is the great grace that helps in the trading for heaven.

You who are traders and go to the Exchange and sell large amounts, you receive only a small payment now. But there is a promise that you will receive great sums of money later. So those who are traders for heaven have some earnest that they are contented with for the present: the firstfruits of the Spirit or perhaps a bare promise from Christ. Yet they know that this promise binds the whole bargain, and they confidently wait for the full payment when they arrive in heaven.

It is a blessed thing when God gives men and women hearts to be willing to trust Him for eternity – to be content with a little comfort and grace now, as a token of the glory that Jesus Christ purchased by His blood and that God promised in His Word. You are not fit to trade for heaven if you cannot trust and be content with the earnest until the promise is fulfilled.

The true trader is willing to wait, satisfied with a little now, while looking for the glory later.

These seven things, put all together, are what make a trader for heaven. This is what it means to have our conversation in heaven.

Chapter 8

Seven Marks of a Life Anchored in Heaven

Now then, there are certain evidences that reveal when a Christian's conversation is truly in heaven. Just as we have already noted the marks of an earthly conversation, so too, there are clear signs that distinguish a heavenly one.

It is certain that some Christians show their conversations are in heaven because **they are able to despise the things of this earth**. If their hearts were not lifted above this world, they would not be able to vilify and think so little of the things of earth. It is proof of the great height of heaven when a man is lifted up very high and looks down on the globe of the earth and sees it as a little speck beneath him. In the same way, it is an evidence that the saints' hearts are on high when they can look on earthly things as small. While we are on the earth, we think the stars are little and the earth is huge, but if we were in heaven, we would see the stars as great and the earth as small.

Paul counted all things as dung and dross, fit only for dogs, compared to *the excellency of the knowledge of Christ Jesus* (Philippians 3:8). Luther called the whole Ottoman Empire just a crumb tossed to the dogs by the great Master of the house.

Surely then, those who so lightly esteem the things of the world have their conversation in heaven.

Another evidence is that **they can be so content with so little in this world yet live such cheerful and comfortable lives**. Many cannot imagine comfort unless they have a certain income and provision. But the godly, those whose hearts are in heaven, can live a joyful and happy life even in physical need. Though they may have only bread and water, poor dwellings, simple clothes, and low esteem in the world, they can still go through life with a joyful heart. They bless God every day, admire, praise, and magnify Him for His rich mercy, and consider their portion to be fair and substantial.

> That they live comfortable lives even without the comforts of this world shows that their conversation is in heaven.

I truly believe that more blessings of God come from the poor, humble people of God in one day than come from the houses of the rich and the noble in forty years. That they live comfortable lives even without the comforts of this world shows that their conversation is in heaven.

Something outside of this world must cause them to rejoice when they can take joy in the lack of these outward things. Men who have earthly hearts, whose joy depends on the things of this world, are undone when they lose their earthly comforts. They have nothing to joy their hearts when they lose the things of the world.

The saints are different. No matter what crosses they bear in this world, they still rejoice in Christ and bless God. Their lives are a continual course of magnifying and praising God for His mercy and goodness to them. Certainly, they have their conversations in heaven.

The faithful described in Hebrews 11 *confessed that they were strangers and pilgrims on the earth. For they that say such things declare plainly that they seek a country* (Hebrews 11:13-14). Surely, there is something else that they are seeking when they treat the things of this world so lightly.

The saints are not fools, so there is some reason they do what they do. They have the same nature you have and the same need of comfort. But they have some comfort that enables them to live comfortably even without the outward things. They are content with just a little, like pilgrims and strangers, declaring plainly that they are seeking another country.

Not only can they live joyfully with little, but they can also suffer the loss of all things – even endure affliction, torment, and torture – with joy. This is an evidence of a heavenly life. The author of Hebrews wrote: *But call to remembrance the former days, in which, after ye were illuminated, ye endured a great fight of afflictions; partly, whilst ye were made a gazingstock both by reproaches and afflictions; and partly, whilst ye became companions of them that were so used. For ye had compassion of me in my bonds, and took joyfully the spoiling of your goods, knowing in yourselves that ye have in heaven a better and an enduring substance* (Hebrews 10:32-34). Knowing their reward was in heaven caused them to endure joyfully the spoiling of their goods. Were they mad to rejoice at the plundering of their estates? No, it was not madness. They rejoiced because they knew in themselves that they had in heaven a better and an enduring substance, and that made them willing to wander about in sheepskins and goatskins, *destitute, afflicted, tormented* (Hebrews 11:37).

If you read the stories of the martyrs, you will find that, often, when they came to the stake, their minds, thoughts, and hearts were in heaven. They encouraged each other with the glory to come, rejoicing even in the flames. Being willing to suffer such hard things for Christ and being able to undergo it all with joy is an evidence that there have been Christians in the world who have had their conversations in heaven.

Another evidence of Christians having their conversations in heaven is that **their hearts are so filled with heavenly riches**. You can know where a man trades by what fills his warehouse. If I enter a man's warehouse and find it filled with Spanish or Turkish goods, I would conclude that he trades in Spain or Turkey. He has the commodities of that country constantly in his warehouse. So it is with the saints: They have the riches of heaven constantly in their hearts. Their hearts are filled with grace, holiness, and the image of God.

Those Christians are filled with spiritual life, and you can see in their faces and their lives the excellency and glory of heaven. Surely his conversation is in heaven who has so much of the riches of heaven in his heart. The Holy Spirit said: *The heart of the wicked is little worth* (Proverbs 10:20). Look into the heart of a wicked man or woman, and you will find filth, lust, and vanity. But look into the hearts of the saints, and you will find God, Christ, the Holy Spirit, and grace. This reveals that they have traded much in heaven. Their hearts are continually filled with grace, and it manifests itself in their lives. Surely, their conversation is in heaven.

Another way this is demonstrated is that **they value the privileges of heaven so highly that they are willing to purchase them at great cost**. Chief among these are the ordinances of God, the wells of salvation. They are the means by which the saints come to enjoy so much of heaven. Without them, their lives cannot be comfortable. Those who are willing to purchase heavenly commodities at so dear a rate as the saints will do, evidently declare their conversations to be in heaven.

Another evidence is that **they are deeply troubled when there is any hindrance in the communion between heaven and their own souls**. If all the ships that sailed from France, Turkey, and Spain to England were stopped, common people would not even be aware of it. But I guarantee you your merchants would know. When they come together at the Exchange, it would be the only thing they talked about. So it is with those who have their conversations in heaven, and in this, there is a great difference between them and those who are earthly-minded. If you tell someone who is consumed with the world that there is a stoppage between them and heaven, they will have no idea what you mean. They will think you are a mad fool.

But the saints are aware of it, and it is a terrible evil to them. When God hides His face from them, when they go into His presence and hear nothing from Him, they mourn deeply. They lament that no letters, as it were, come from heaven. If the mail does not arrive from a country, merchants are troubled. So when saints send up their prayers to heaven but no answer comes down, when they cannot feel the influence of grace on their souls, they bewail this as the greatest evil that could befall them. That God seems to be a stranger to them is greater than any worldly loss. They complain of these things to one another and sigh until communion is restored. This plainly declares that they are traders for heaven and that their conversations are there.

> The saints show their heavenly conversation by their willingness to die.

Last, the saints show their heavenly conversation by their willingness to die. When the time comes to depart this world, they often go with comfort, joy, peace, and triumph. Many of the saints are ready to die and rejoice at the hope of eternal life. If they had not conversed in heaven while they lived here, their souls would not have been so willing to leave their bodies.

A man with no business in another country dreads going there; but one who has traded there and grown rich there, looks forward to the journey. Whatever he is in his own country, he is a great man there. How glad he is when the ship he is on catches a fair wind and brings him quickly to that country. So it is with the saints who have their conversations in heaven.

Because they have so many riches there, they die with joy and bless God. The day of their death is the most blessed day, for they are now going to the country that they have been trading to all of their days and where their true riches lie.

These, then, are the evidences and demonstrations that the saints have their conversations in heaven.

Chapter 9

Why the Saints' Hearts Are Set on Heaven

But now, if you ask the reason why the saints have their conversations in heaven, I answer briefly with these four reasons:

The Soul's Heavenly Origin

The first reason is because their souls, which are their better part, are from heaven. You know that when God made man, He breathed into his nostrils the breath of life. The soul of man is, as it were, the very breath of God. God did not say of man's soul, as He did of other creatures, "Let it be made; let there be a soul in man's body." No, when He had formed the body, He breathed the soul into it. This shows that the soul of man has a more heavenly and divine origin than any of the other creatures in this world.

And because the soul's origin is so divine and heavenly, when it is set at liberty, it longs to return to its origin. Indeed, though man's soul is of a divine and heavenly nature, through the fall of man it has become so corrupted that it is almost turned to flesh. It is so mixed with fleshly and unclean things that it seems almost to have lost its original glory. That is why a natural man is called *flesh*: *That which is born of the flesh is flesh* (John 3:6) – as if he had no soul at all. For through man's fall, the nature of the soul appears to have changed. It is so degraded that it seems as if it never had such a divine and heavenly beginning.

But when God works grace in the soul, the soul of man begins to return to itself, to know itself, and to recover something of the nature it had at creation. And as soon as the soul begins to know itself, it immediately looks on all the things are here below as vile and contemptible – for indeed, all the things of this world are infinitely beneath the soul of man. The soul of man is near to God Himself. Therefore, when the soul returns to its true nature, it desires to be somewhere other than where it is and to converse with those things that are suited to its original.

> When God works grace in the soul, the soul of man begins to return to itself

It is as with a man of noble birth: Suppose a prince, carried away into another country while still a child, is raised as a slave and made to rake ditches and other low tasks. All the while that he is there, he knows nothing about his origin and only cares about getting enough food to eat and getting his work done. But if he learns where he is from and who he truly is – that he was born heir to a great prince or emperor who dwells in glory in another land – then the thoughts and longing of the one who lived as a slave would be in the country of his birth. If he could be there, he would be so happy! It would cheer him just to hear someone speak of that country.

So it is with the souls of men. They are the offspring of the Most High God, breathed into man by the great King of heaven and earth. Now through man's fall, the soul has been enslaved to the devil and made to work providing for the flesh. But when God converts the soul, the Lord says to the man or woman,

"You are born from on high. Your soul is (as it were) a spark of the divine. Not only is God your Father by creation, but by an even more special work than the first creation, your soul is from God and is of a divine nature so that it is capable of communion with the Father, Son, and Holy Spirit." Certainly, such a soul was never meant to delight merely in the flesh, to live for nothing but eating and drinking for a short while!

Oh, consider your country – the place from which you came. This is one great work of grace: to make us know the excellence of our souls and from where they came. And surely, when grace does this, it must turn the hearts of the converted to God and cause their conversation to be in heaven.

The Gift of a Divine Nature

The second reason why the saints have their conversation in heaven is not only because the soul has a heavenly origin and therefore cannot be satisfied with a portion in this world, but also because, when grace comes, the soul receives a divine nature beyond what it had even in its first creation.

The apostle Peter said, *According as his divine power hath given unto us all things that pertain unto life and godliness, through the knowledge of him that hath called us to glory and virtue: whereby are given unto us exceeding great and precious promises: that by these ye might be partakers of the divine nature* (2 Peter 1:3-4). Certainly Peter did not mean merely what Adam had in innocence, for I never read that Adam's soul in innocence is called a "divine nature." It is true that in conversion man is renewed after the image of God, but there is more than this: The Holy Spirit comes to dwell in the soul in a higher way than it ever dwelled in the soul of Adam at first.

Before, man was a creature only, having relation to God as his Creator. But now, the believer is made one with Christ, the second person of the Trinity, and through Him, one with the Father. Thus the soul is raised to a higher nature than man ever had in innocence. Scripture says of Adam: *The first man is of the earth, earthy* (1 Corinthians 15:47). Even in his innocence, in comparison with the second Adam, Adam was still of the earth, earthy. Had Adam stood, his posterity would have been of the earth, earthy, as well, and their happiness limited to this earth. We never read in Scripture of a heavenly condition Adam would have been in if he had stood.

But the second Adam is the *Lord from heaven*, heavenly (1 Corinthians 15:47). And His posterity – those who by regeneration are made the children of the everlasting Father, who are made the posterity of Jesus Christ by faith – are likewise from heaven, heavenly.

Therefore, in regeneration, the souls of believers are induced with a divine nature, with such high principles of grace as must lift their souls to heaven. It is as if a lump of earth were changed into a bird: It would at once fly into the air. So it is in the work of conversion: All men and women are earthly and sink naturally down to the earth as their center. But when grace converts them, a spirit is put into them, and they rise toward heaven. It is not more natural for earth to fall down low than it is for fire and air to ascend up high because every creature moves toward its center. Just as heavy things fall down toward their proper place and light things rise upward to theirs, the conversations of the saints must be in heaven because heaven is their proper center and is the place suitable to the divine nature put into them.

The Saints' Treasures Are Above

The saints' conversations must be in heaven because the things that are the most precious to them are there. I will list many of those precious things here:

- Their Father, God, is in heaven: *Our Father which art in heaven* (Matthew 6:9).

- Jesus Christ is in heaven: *Seek those things which are above, where Christ sitteth on the right hand of God* (Colossians 3:1).

- Jesus Christ, their Head, is in heaven.

- Their Husband is in heaven.

- Their Elder Brother is in heaven.

- Their King is in heaven.

- Their treasure is in heaven (Matthew 6:20).

- Their inheritance is in heaven (1 Peter 1:4).

- Their hope is in heaven (Colossians 1:5).

- Their mansion is in heaven (John 14:2).

- Their best friends are in heaven.

- Their substance is in heaven (Hebrews 10:34).

- Their reward is in heaven (Matthew 5:12).

- Their wages are in heaven.

Since all these things are in heaven, it makes sense that their conversations are there also. And they are going to heaven. Now that they are traveling that way, their hearts will be there. Here they are just a while, pilgrims and strangers, but they will soon be in their everlasting home: *Then we which are alive and remain shall be caught up together with them in the clouds, to meet the Lord in the air: and so shall we ever be with the Lord* (1 Thessalonians 4:17).

They already have much of heaven within them. Scripture says: *The kingdom of God is within you* (Luke 17:21). Eternal life has already begun in the saints, so it is natural for their conversations to be there. The author of Hebrews wrote: *Knowing in yourselves that ye have in heaven a better and an enduring substance* (Hebrews 10:34); but it can also be read, "Knowing that you have heaven – a better and enduring substance in yourselves." That way, the words *knowing in yourselves* do not only refer to what they know by hearsay – though this is true; you can know heaven by hearsay. They hear their pastors speak of heaven and read it in the Word of God – but they also know it in themselves. They know it because God has revealed it in their own hearts. Even if they cannot read and never hear another sermon, they know by what is revealed in themselves *that they have a better and an enduring substance.* That is the truth. But the words may be more proper to the original read this way: *Knowing, that you have heaven in yourselves, a better and enduring substance.* Eternal life is already begun in the hearts of the saints; therefore, it is no wonder that their conversations are in heaven.

God Weans His People from the World

The last reason why the saints have their conversations in heaven is because God has ordered the affairs of this world in such a way as to wean the hearts of His saints from the world. God loves to have the hearts of His people in heaven where He has stored up such glorious things for them. But because the saints here in the world have so much of the world in them, they would romanticize living here in the world; therefore God orders things so that they find little contentment in this world. They are weary of the world and are wearied by it. It is the reason why God's people have so many crosses to bear in this world and why He has kept them so low and common in the world.

Do not draw the wrong conclusion that God does not love

you because He keeps you so low and you bear crosses that others do not. Oh! That is not true! It is because He does love you that He gathers your hearts to heaven and weans you from the world. Because you are absent from Him here in this world, God wants you to long to be with Him in heaven and wants the full stream of your affections to run after those things you will have with Him in heaven. That is the correct use you are to make of those afflictions you meet and those crosses that befall you in this world – they remind you that your true life and portion is not here but in heaven.

Chapter 10

A Warning to Those Living as Citizens of Hell

We have spoken at length about a heavenly conversation and have explained in detail what that heavenly life is and what it consists of. But now it is time to apply these truths. All along, I have tried not only to speak to your minds but also to reach your hearts – seeking to quicken my words so that I may quicken your hearts. From the whole matter, then, there are several lessons that may be profitable to you.

The first is this: If the saints live the kinds of heavenly lives that have been described to you, then how far from being saints – how far from being godly – are those whose conversations are in hell! There is a kind of men who profess themselves to be Christians, who say they hope to go to heaven, yet if you look at their lives, they are the very lives of hell. In the end, it is not what men say but how they live that will decide their portion. He who belongs to heaven has his conversation in heaven, and he who belongs to hell has his conversation in hell.

Now, what is the conversation of hell? What is done there? Blaspheming and cursing. What is there in hell but hatred and malice? What is there in hell but raging and filthiness? These very things mark the lives of many men who are little better than devils incarnate. In many households, the name of God is blasphemed. There is cursing, railing, malice, wrath, and pride. And though they live here in this world, they live out the life of the place to which they truly belong.

Just as the saints, whose conversations in heaven, go at death to their own place – that is, to heaven, where their lives were already centered – so on the contrary, the wicked, whose conversations are in hell, go at death to their own place. As it was said of Judas, he went *to his own place* (Acts 1:25), so it is with every wicked man. Dying, he goes to his own place. He had his conversation in hell while he lived, so that is his proper place. He found contentment and delight in the things that were done there, so when he dies, there he must go. *Where the tree falleth, there it shall be* (Ecclesiastes 11:3). As your conversation is and where the bent of your heart is, so it will remain for all eternity.

Chapter 11

A Warning to Hypocrites Who Claim Heaven but Live for Earth

The second application also rebukes hypocrites. There are openly wicked and profane people who have their conversations in hell. But there is another kind of men – unsound professors of Christ, hypocrites – and their conversations hover between heaven and earth. Their conduct is not wholly heavenly or hellish or even entirely earthly, but something in between. Sometimes they seem to be high above – sometimes very zealous in their claim of Christianity, fervent in their duties and religious talk. But at other times, they sink as low as any worldly spirit and even reveal much of hell in their hearts and in their ways.

They claim to be the seed of Abraham, but they are not like the stars of heaven. They are more like meteors that flash between heaven and earth. We call them "blazing stars," but they are not as bright as the stars, nor are they of the same heavenly nature as the stars. They are formed from unclean vapors from the earth, and rising near the heavens, make a show of themselves as if they were some star in heaven. A child would think a blazing star is much bigger than one of the stars that is one hundred times larger.

But meteors are different. In just a little while, they fall, vanish, and come to nothing. So it is with many hypocrites. By the Word, they are raised up and seem to be above the stars. They put on a glittering show as if they have something heavenly in them, even like the stars of heaven. They may seem, for a time, to be more heavenly than the truly godly.

They astonish others with their fine parts and impressive abilities. They may speak eloquently about heavenly things. You may find some with no soundness at all, but they speak excellently using the very language of Canaan – but only in settings where it gains them respect. They are meteors that hang between heaven and earth. Their words and outward actions make them appear lofty and heavenly, but the truth is that their hearts are still groveling on the earth. Many times, while they have the most moving prayers, God sees their hearts clinging to some base, earthly thing. Their hearts, which seem to be so heavenly, are set on the world.

They are like a hawk that soars high as if it were an eagle, but all the while, its eye is fixed on some carrion below. At the first chance, it swoops upon the prey – for that is what it truly desires. So it is with the hypocrite: Though he rises high in some actions, his eye is always on some earthly gain. When the opportunity comes, down he goes, and that is where he truly delights to be. Though his conduct may seem heavenly for a time, he will never reach the heavens where the saints go. He will fall and sink down to hell forever.

Chapter 12

Why We Should Not Complain Against the Narrow Way of God

The third application is this: Since the saints' true way of life is a heavenly life, we should be ashamed to find fault with strictness in the ways of God. Do not speak against holiness as though it were too severe. Do not say, "Why must we be so careful, so precise, so pure? Why must we labor so much?" Tell me – can you possibly live a life more holy than a heavenly life?

Some people speak very worldly when they say, "Well, we cannot be saints – we are not saints." But Scripture says otherwise: The Holy Spirit calls all believers saints, even those who have the smallest degree of true grace. Some say, "When we get to heaven, then we will live better; but while we are in this world, we cannot." Yet the Word of God disagrees: While you are here in this world, your conversation – your way of life – is to be in heaven.

Surely such people either do not know the Word or they deliberately close their eyes against it. The Scriptures plainly command us: *Be ye therefore perfect, even as your Father which is in heaven is perfect* (Matthew 5:48). It is a strange and startling command, but it is the command of Christ Himself. We are told to walk as Christ walked (1 John 2:6) and that *every man that hath this hope in him purifieth himself, even as he is pure* (1 John 3:3). And finally, it declares, "Our conversation is in heaven."

Put all these together: Be perfect as your Father is perfect. Walk as Christ walked. Purify yourselves as He is pure. Let your conversation be in heaven. What do all these point to, except a life of real holiness and strictness?

This shows that the work of a Christian here in this world is no idle, lazy, or sluggish life. You who call yourselves Christians need to get moving. Awaken those drowsy, heavy hearts if such things are required of you – that you should be holy as God is holy, pure as Christ is pure, and heavenly in your very way of living. Surely, this demands great energy and life in the hearts of Christians.

Therefore, do not rest content with mere profession, doing some small religious duties, or with just being a little better than others. Aim for heaven. Look up there and make that your pattern.

Chapter 13

When Godly People Fall Short in Living a Heavenly Life

The fourth application to us is that being told our conversation should be in heaven is a rebuke even to those who are truly godly – for many of them fail greatly in this matter. Their way of life is too low, too earthly. If they were to examine their hearts honestly, they could not say that their conversations are in heaven. David said, *I am a stranger in the earth* (Psalm 119:19). But many Christians could say, "I am a stranger to heaven."

Earth should be the place of our pilgrimage and heaven our true home, but for many, it is the reverse: Heaven is the place where they feel like strangers, and earth is the place they call home. They send a thought up now and then to heaven, as now and then men will look up toward heaven – but where are their hearts? Where is the main activity of their spirits?

The Lord Himself said, *The heaven is my throne, and the earth is my footstool* (Isaiah 66:1). Spiritual things, such as the throne of God, are to be looked on as the good things and the earthly things only as the things of God's footstool. But many live as if earth were their throne and heaven only their footstool! They make heavenly things subordinate to earthly things. Oh! This should not be in any of those who claim to be Christians. None of the saints should rest content until they can say, "Praise God! Even though He lets me live on the earth, my conversation is in heaven."

What an unworthy and shameful thing it is for one who professes to have his inheritance in heaven to have his heart so mingled here with the earth. When Joseph sent for his father, Jacob, he told him, *Regard not your stuff; for the good of all the land of Egypt is yours* (Genesis 45:20). Regard not the stuff; do not let it grieve you to forsake your stuff. Leave it all behind you, for all the good things of Egypt are yours. How shameful that Christians regard their stuff as much as they do when they have the hope of all the good things, not of Egypt but of heaven itself!

If we have truly seen the things of heaven, the things of earth should appear dark and dull in comparison. As Paul said, *That which was made glorious had no glory in this respect, by reason of the glory that excelleth* (2 Corinthians 3:10). He was speaking of comparing the law and the gospel. The law came with glory, but compared to the gospel, it had none at all. In the gospel we are, *with open face, beholding as in a glass the glory of God* (2 Corinthians 3:18) and are changed into the same image from glory to glory.

But we may apply it this way: The things of the earth that were glorious before in your eyes, in comparison of the greater glory, should not at all be glorious. Before conversion, these things were glorious, and there is some kind of glory in the things of this world. They are gilded and varnished over, but in comparison of the greater glory, they are not glorious at all. This makes sense for those who have never seen anything more glorious than the things of the world, but you who have seen the greater glory should not count these things glorious.

Oh, Christians, lift up your hearts to heaven and let your conversations be there! True, God has ordered it that we must live here a while, and we must be content. Indeed, for some believers who have their conversations in heaven, it is part of their self-denial and their subjection to God to be willing to live on the earth until God's time comes. This is a mystery to many – that even if we were kings here, wearing crowns of gold, it would still be a kind of obedience and self-denial to be willing to stay here. We might come to attain this if our conversations and hearts were in heaven.

> Oh, Christians, lift up your hearts to heaven and let your conversations be there!

Consider Daniel: Though he was exiled in Babylon and could not live in Jerusalem where the temple was, he still opened his window toward the city of God, ever looking that way. So must we, though God has not yet brought us bodily to the heavenly Jerusalem, open the windows and doors of our hearts toward heaven.

I remember the story of Edward I, King of England. He longed to travel to Jerusalem, but death prevented him. So he commanded his son to carry his heart there after his death. So it should be with us: We should endeavor to have our hearts there and to have as much of heaven as we can though we cannot be there ourselves in nature.

God has placed into every creature an instinct to move to its proper place. Fire, because the proper place of fire is above, will always rise. And the proper place of earth is below; therefore, it will fall down to the center, even if it breaks itself in falling. And so it will be with a Christian: Though he breaks himself to pieces, whatsoever he suffers, he has an instinct to carry him upward to his proper place. If you try to restrain fire, it will break forth with great force to get upward. That is why guns have such force. There is restrained fire in the powder. Because the fire needs to get above, when the powder is fired, it breaks with violence. If it cannot have vent to get out, it breaks anything in the world, for it must get out so that it may get up to its own place.

A Christian, too, should have strong impetus to get up to his own place. That would be an evidence indeed that heaven is his proper place. O Christians, lift up your hearts and let your conversations be in heaven.

Chapter 14

A Heavenly Life Is a Powerful Witness

I do not need to explain again what heavenly conversation is – you have already heard it fully opened. But to press this exhortation upon your heart, consider this first:

A heavenly life is a convincing life. When they see you living heavenly, people will be convinced that you have something more than they do. The men of the world know the things of the world – those are the things their hearts are on and what occupies their minds. But now, when they see Christians just as entangled with the earth as they are, they conclude that Christians live by the same principles that they do.

But a truly heavenly conversation convinces. When others see them walking above the world with a steadiness and proportion for the whole course of their lives, when in all situations they carry themselves as men who belong to another world, then people know something is different. A man may, for a time, disguise himself as a native in a foreign land, but sooner or later, those who were born in that place will detect that he is a stranger. In the same way, it is very difficult for those who do not have true grace to carry themselves as if they do. Though they may appear to be heavenly for a time, true citizens of heaven will discern that they do not truly have grace. The truth is that even worldly men will betray themselves as children of the earth because their speech will betray them.

But when Christians walk steadily with their hearts and conversations in heaven, their very lives become convincing. They have the bright rays of heaven around them, and the luster of heaven shines no matter where they go or who they are with.

> Worldly men will betray themselves as children of the earth because their speech will betray them.

The consciences of men will be forced to say, "These people are certainly the citizens of heaven. They seem to be in heaven continually. If there are any on earth who belong to the New Jerusalem, it must be these people."

It is said of the martyr Dr. Taylor that he rejoiced to be imprisoned because he was then in the company of that "angel of God," Mr. Bradford. Mr. Bradford's conversation was as an angel of heaven. Mr. Bradford's life was so holy, so angelic that it convicted people everywhere he went.[1] What a blessing it is when Christians live such convincing lives!

You remember the rich man in torment who begged Abraham to send someone from the dead to warn his brothers so they would not have to join him where he was. Abraham replied, *They have Moses and the prophets.* But the man insisted: *If one went unto them from the dead, they will repent.* If God would send one from heaven to live among men and preach to them, surely, they would pay attention to him. Would it not be a great benefit to the world if God were to send some saint or angel from heaven to converse in a physical way among us?

Christians should live like that. They should live as if they came straight from heaven after talking with God every day.

---

[1] This story refers to Rowland Taylor and John Bradford. Dr. Taylor was martyred defending clerical marriage, and Mr. Bradford was killed for preaching Protestant theology.

When they go to God in the morning, they should strive and not rest until they have gotten alone with God – their hearts in heaven and themselves on the mount of communion with Him. Then, when they come down, their families will know by the shine of their faces and the way that they live that they have been with God that day.

Now I ask you: Do you live in such a way that your family and your neighbors can tell you have been with God in heaven this morning? If we began each day with real communion with heaven, our lives would be convincing all day long, and they would be profitable to the world and of great use in the places where they live.

It is written of Christ that when He ascended up to heaven, He gave gifts to men (Ephesians 4:8). If we more often ascended in our hearts to heaven, we would be more able to bless and benefit those around us.

Chapter 15

A Heavenly Life Keeps Growing

A heavenly conversation is a growing conversation. Believers who walk this way grow quickly in grace. In a short time, they thrive and attain a great measure of communion with God the Father and with Jesus Christ. Every day they grow more and more spiritual, having so much of heaven within them.

It is true that when they come into heaven, they will be made perfect. But now, their growth depends on what they draw from heaven. It is the influence of heaven that makes them flourish. Suppose the soil where flowers and herbs grow is very fertile, and the plants themselves are firmly rooted in the earth. Yet if the heavens have no influence on them – if there is no sunshine or rain – then they will not grow much, if at all. They will quickly wither.

So it is with Christians. No matter how much assistance they have here to help them grow, no matter how many ordinances – if they do not have the rich dews from heaven, they will not grow. If they do grow at all, they will bear little or no fruit. And what fruit they do produce will be shriveled and sour.

Fruit that receives the most sunlight grows riper and sweeter than other fruit. Fruit that grows in the shade, shielded from the beams of heaven, turns out sour. The reason that the saints have so little and such sour fruit is because they have such little influence from heaven. They do not stand in the open Sun, their souls are not presented daily to God to have the warm beams of the Sun of Righteousness shine from heaven on them. Something stands between heaven and their souls.

But when a Christian's conversation is truly in heaven, it becomes not only a convincing conversation but also a growing conversation.

Chapter 16

A Heavenly Life Brings Glory to God

A heavenly conversation is a conversation that glorifies God much. God would receive so much glory from such a life! *Let your light so shine before men, that they may see your good works, and glorify your Father which is in heaven* (Matthew 5:16).

When men and women live with their hearts on heaven, the image of the God of heaven is displayed in them. The Lord delights to have His glory spread abroad through His saints, sending reflections of it into the world. Just as a mirror can catch the beams of the sun and reflect them on a wall, so the saints, by their heavenly conversation, can take the beams of the glory of God and reflect them on the world and on the faces of men. The hearts of the saints should be as a glass taking the beams of the glory of God and casting them up and down where they are – so that your heavenly Father might be glorified through them.

Let every Christian ask: "What glory do I bring to God by my life? Do others glorify God when they see the brightness of the holiness of God in me? Do they see a reason to bless God because they see so much of the glory of God in me?"

Certainly, more of the glory of God shines in the gracious, holy, spiritual conversation of a Christian than shines in the sun, moon, stars, and earth. The works of creation and providence that are in heaven and earth: the creatures that God made in the heavens – the sun, moon, and stars – and here in this world – the seas, the earth, the plants – they have much of the glory of God, but a heavenly conversation declares more of the glory of God than all these. The psalmist said, *The heavens declare the glory of God; and the firmament sheweth his handywork* (Psalm 19:1). But this is even more true of the heavenly lives of the saints. They declare the glory of God. Those who shine in the firmament of the church are stars, for the church is God's firmament, and His saints shine there as lights declaring His handiwork.

Now it is true that in heaven one star differs from another star in glory, and so it is among Christians: Not every believer can attain the same measure of glory as another. Yet every one of them is a star. The least Christian, the weakest believer, should still shine in the firmament of the church. Though he cannot shine as gloriously as the Sun or as other stars, there should never be a believer, never a godly man or woman in the church, who should fail to shine at all. Each should be as the gospel: a mirror in which we may see the glory of God, in whom His glory may be seen, as it were, with an open face.

A heavenly conversation, then, is a life that glorifies God.

Chapter 17

A Heavenly Life Brings Honor to the Saints

A heavenly conversation is also one that will bring great glory to ourselves. Though it is true that the saints should aim at the glory of God most, glory will inevitably come to them as well if their lives are lived in heaven. It is impossible for believers to walk in a heavenly conversation without being honored, even in the consciences of men.

Scripture reveals that when we glorify God, we also glorify ourselves: *Wherefore also we pray always for you, that our God would count you worthy of this calling, and fulfil all the good pleasure of his goodness, and the work of faith with power: that the name of our Lord Jesus Christ may be glorified in you, and ye in him, according to the grace of our God and the Lord Jesus Christ* (2 Thessalonians 1:11-12).

Paul prayed for the Thessalonians that they might live so filled with the grace of God that the name of the Lord Jesus Christ would be glorified in them. This is what every saint should desire and strive for – that the name of Christ may be glorified in them. The text adds, *and ye in him.* Labor, then, that Christ may be glorified in your lives, and you will be glorified in Him.

We should desire that Christ may have glory in our glory, and then we will have glory in Christ's glory. This is a sweet and blessed life – when saints have such hearts as to say, "Lord, let me have no glory except that in it you may be glorified." Then the Lord replies, "Is it so? Do you desire no further glory in this world for yourself except that I may be glorified in it? Then I will have no glory in this world except what you shall share in."

Christ will make us partakers of His glory, just as we make Him partaker of our glory. A heavenly conversation that glorifies God will glorify the saints too.

Chapter 18

A Heavenly Life Makes Suffering Easier

A heavenly conversation will make all sufferings very easy. It will be nothing to endure whatever trials you meet in this world if your conversation is in heaven. All reviling, reproaches, and wrongs will seem as nothing if your life is lived above. You will despise all these things that the men of the world think are such great matters. Men who have conversed in heaven will not be very troubled by the sufferings of earth.

Paul wrote: *For our light affliction, which is but for a moment, worketh for us a far more exceeding and eternal weight of glory; while we look not at the things which are seen, but at the things which are not seen: for the things which are seen are temporal; but the things which are not seen are eternal* (2 Corinthians 4:17-18). Afflictions are light when our eye is above all these things.

Consider a remarkable passage in the gospels concerning Christ's transfiguration on the mount. There He showed His glory to the disciples that He brought with Him – Peter, James, and John. Compare that story with that of Christ being in His agony in Gethsemane, which happened soon after. His soul was heavy unto death. He was about to be betrayed and then crucified the next day. He fell groveling on the ground and sweat great drops of blood because of the anguish that was upon His spirit, and He cried out: *O my Father, if it be possible, let this cup pass from me* (Matthew 26:39). What a vast difference there is between Christ in His agony and Christ on the mount in His transfiguration!

Notice that Christ did not allow all the disciples to see Him in His agony. Only Peter, James, and John, the three who had seen His glory on the mount, saw Him in His agony. Why? Because those who have seen Christ in His glory can endure to see Him in His agony without stumbling. But the others, who did not see Christ in His glory in His transfiguration, might have been offended if they had seen Him in such distress: "Is this our Lord and Master that is in such anguish?"

But those who saw Him glorified were not offended: "Even though He is in agony now, we know Him to be a glorious Savior, and we will believe and trust in Him still." The lesson is that those who fellowship often with Christ in glory and can see heaven are able to bear the sight of His agony, or of any sufferings in themselves, without harm.

Stephen, when stones were hurled about his head, looked up and saw the heavens opened, and it was nothing to him then. He fell asleep, rejoicing in the expectation of heaven. And you can read in the Book of Martyrs that many, when brought to their sufferings, rejoiced when they thought of heaven and eternal life. One woman, seeing her child ready to be burned, was expected by the crowd to wring her hands and lament bitterly, watching her child stepping into the flames. Instead, she simply said to him, "Remember eternal life, my son." To converse much with heaven makes all the sufferings of this world seem as nothing.

Chapter 19

A Heavenly Life Brings Joy

Then – oh, the sweetness and comfort that there will be while the soul is conversing in heaven! Oh, the joy and the peace that come with the clear evidence that the soul shares in the death, resurrection, and intercession of Jesus Christ! Those whose conversations are in heaven gain by this a sure witness in their own souls that they have a portion in Christ's death, in His resurrection, in His ascension, and in His intercession – and this is comfort enough.

Consider this: *If ye then be risen with Christ, seek those things which are above, where Christ sitteth on the right hand of God. Set your affection on things above, not on things on the earth. For ye are dead, and your life is hid with Christ in God. When Christ, who is our life, shall appear, then shall ye also appear with him in glory* (Colossians 3:1-4). This is evidence that you are risen with Christ, that you are dead to the world, that you have an interest in His ascension, are partakers of His resurrection, and share in His intercession.

Those who now have their conversations in heaven may know certainly that they have passed from death to life and that when Christ ascended, He went to heaven to take possession for them. They are, in Him, already in heaven where Christ is: *And hath raised us up together, and made us sit together in heavenly places together in Christ Jesus* (Ephesians 2:6).

For He is there as our common Head, and they are, in that sense, ascended with Christ already. Christ is there as an Advocate, making intercession for them to the Father. These are the consolations of those whose conversations are in heaven.

Chapter 20

A Heavenly Life Is Secure

A life lived in heaven is a very safe life – you will be free from snares and temptations. An earthly conversation always subjects us to temptation, but a heavenly conversation delivers us from it. When is the bird in danger of the lime twig or the net except when she comes down to feed on the ground? If she could always keep herself above, she would be safe from both the snare and the net.

Chrysostom uses this same picture: "Keep above, and you will be free from the fowler's trap." A heavenly conversation is a safe conversation.

Chapter 21

A Heavenly Life Opens Wide the Gates of Glory

A heavenly conversation will lead to an abundant entrance into the kingdom of heaven. When such believers come to die, how joyfully they will die! What an abundant and open welcome they will have into the everlasting kingdom of our Lord and Savior Jesus Christ. For when they die, they only change their place, not their company. They simply go to their Father's house to partake of the mansions Christ has already prepared.

Friends, work to keep your conversations in heaven. And remember, this is not something reserved only for the most eminent Christians but for all Christians. See how Paul presses this upon the Thessalonians: *As you know how we exhorted and comforted and charged every one of you, as a Father doth his children, that ye would walk worthy of God, who hath called you unto his kingdom and glory* (1 Thessalonians 2:11-12). That is, you are to live in a way that reflects the glorious kingdom of God to which you have been called. According to such a high calling, we should walk worthy of it – for this is what God requires of us.

It is said of Christ – speaking of Himself: *the Son of man which is in heaven* (John 3:13). It should be said of every child of God, not only that they *will* one day go to heaven, but that even now, in a very real sense, they are already *in* heaven.

Chapter 22

How to Grow in a Heavenly Life

But you may ask, "How can we live with our minds and lives set on heaven? It sounds excellent, but how will we be able to do it?"

Believe It Is Possible

Be persuaded that it is attainable. Christians should settle this with themselves: I can live a life of heaven while I am on the earth. Knowing there is such a thing and believing it is possible will stir up the spirit of a Christian to pursue it. I may live in heaven here, with God, Christ, His angels, and saints. Others before us have attained it.

How? Not by their own strength. They were men and women subject to the same weaknesses that you and I are. Even Paul himself, who had his conversation in heaven, struggled with sin. But through the strength of Christ, he could do all things (Philippians 4:13). He was nothing in himself. In Romans, Paul even said that he was *sold under sin*, and when he would do good, evil was present with him (Romans 7:14, 19, 21). He was led captive, and he found a law in his members warring against the law of his mind (Romans 7:23). He was not free from corruption, and God allowed him *a thorn in the flesh, the messenger of Satan* to humble him (2 Corinthians 12:7).

And yet, by the strength of Christ, Paul learned to live a heavenly life. And not only that, Paul wrote to the Philippians – a spiritual church but a poor and ordinary church, not gifted like the Corinthians were – and said they, too, had their conversation in heaven. Therefore, it is indeed attainable.

Keep a Clear Conscience

If you want your life to reflect heaven, labor to keep your conscience clean. Keep heaven in your conscience. Those people who fully defile their consciences lose their fellowship with heaven; the presence of the God of heaven becomes burdensome to them. Once they have defiled their consciences, they hate to be in His presence. *If there is a hell in a man's conscience, there will not be a heaven in his conversation.* But if they labor to keep heaven in their consciences, to keep them pure and clean, then there will be a heaven in their lives.

Seize Opportunities for Heavenly Practices

Though you are busy in this world, watch for opportunities to lift your soul to heaven. You who are servants, do not neglect your master's work, for even that can be service to God. Yet, within your duties, look for opportunities – even short ones – for prayer, meditation, Scripture reading, for conversing with God. If you cannot take long hours, take many shorter moments. We would find them if we would just watch. Those who diligently watch for opportunities for heavenly exercises and value them are the men and women who will come to attain a heavenly conversation. They will not treat having fellowship with God a light matter – as if it makes no difference whether they pray or not. Christians who want their conversations in heaven will look for and value these opportunities, for in them lies the joy and comfort of their lives.

Beware of Formality

If you desire a heavenly life, be careful not to rest in formality. Watch for your opportunities, but do not use them just to get your duty done and over with. This will greatly darken your conversations. They will be earthly, not heavenly, and there will be no beauty at all in them if you come to rest in formality in holy performances.

There are many Christians that we hope may have a good root in grace, yet because they practice a routine religion, they bring little honor to Christ and find little comfort for their own souls. They go on in a dull and lifeless manner, never knowing what it means to have communion with God.

Oh, be careful! This is a danger for all of us because we are all by nature subject to it. Even when our consciences are enlightened and they drive us to prayer or worship, the devil comes in to add his temptations to the corruptions of our own hearts. When we have done our task, we think, "I have done it. It is over. I prayed." But were you really in heaven? Did you converse with God? Beware of formality, for it will hinder your conversation.

> Beware of formality, for it will hinder your conversation.

Even the weakest Christian can chatter to God with broken words and half sentences, yet if he does not rest in formality, he may have much real communion with God. Meanwhile, those with excellent abilities, if they rest in formality and are content to just get the task done, will never know what it means to have a conversation in heaven.

Discipline the Body

Learn to discipline your bodies. Do not make provision for the flesh or indulge its lusts (Romans 13:14). How did Paul come to have his conversation in heaven? He said that he beat down his body (1 Corinthians 9:27). The Greek word paints the picture of bruising it black and blue. He clubbed it down. He meant that this body of his would drag his heart away from spiritual things and make him earthly and sensual, so he had to master it. He would not give that satisfaction to the flesh and body so as to strengthen any temptation that would draw his heart away from spiritual and heavenly things. No Christian can live a heavenly life without carefully watching over his senses and desires while he lives here. If we learn, like Paul, to beat down the body, we may rise to have our conversation in heaven.

Draw Strength through Christ, the Ladder to Heaven

Learn the mystery of godliness – that all your strength must be drawn from Jesus Christ in everything you do. For Christ is Jacob's Ladder. Remember when Jacob dreamed he saw a ladder reaching up to heaven on which angels ascended and descended (Genesis 28:12)? Jesus Christ is Jacob's ladder to Christians. If you want to reach heaven, it must be by Him.

There is such an infinite gulf between God and us that unless we have Christ to mediate for us, we can never come to God, and God cannot come to us. We must be instructed in the mystery of the gospel in conversing with God through a mediator. Christ the Mediator is the only ladder. We do not need to go up to heaven to bring Christ down – we can have Christ in our hearts, set Him up, and go up to heaven by His mediation.

What we expect from God, we should expect to receive it through Christ, and what we offer to God, we present through the hand and heart of Christ. Those who are acquainted with this have much communion with heaven.

Even though no unclean thing may go to heaven, by Jesus Christ the Mediator, I may come up there and present myself, for God looks on the saints through Him as righteous. Clothed with His righteousness, believers may come to their Father with boldness, having their Elder Brother's garments on them. They may come and kneel before the throne of grace. They can come into God's presence and kneel every morning to ask for their Father's blessing. It is by Christ that we have access to the Father.

Acquaint yourself with the mystery of godliness in drawing all from Christ and offering all to God through Christ. By Christ, Jacob's Ladder, is how heaven comes down to us and how we climb up to heaven.

But many approach God only in a natural way: "All blessings come from God; therefore, I will ask Him for today's needs." And they serve God because their consciences tell them they must worship and serve Him while they live here – but in a dull, lifeless way.

All good comes from God through a Mediator, through Jesus Christ, the second person of the Trinity, the God-Man, and all my service is offered up to God through Him. The Mediator God-Man unites God and me together, so by Him, I have acceptance both for my person and all my actions. By Him, I receive other blessings than those that come from God merely as Creator. God bountifully bestows many good things on His creation, but when we come to deal with God in Christ, we are given heavenly blessings. These blessings are supernatural – beyond the power of nature, even beyond all those blessings that nature can be any conduit of. They enjoy God in Christ and so come to enjoy God in a heavenly, supernatural way.

This is the way to have our conversations in heaven. Those Christians who are better acquainted with the gospel of Christ, come to live far more heavenly conversations than others that go on in a dull, heavy, and natural kind of way of serving God. Not being acquainted with this mystery, their hearts lie low upon the earth and do not know what it is to have their conversations in heaven.

Live by Faith

The last directive I will give for living a heavenly life is to exercise much faith. Faith is the grace that lifts us above the creature and above nature. Many Christians think they must exercise love for God and exercise sorrow for sin. Those are good, along with the grace of repentance, mourning for sin, and patience. But the great grace that is to be employed if you want to attain a heavenly life is the exercise of faith.

Be diligent to use that grace much, for it is by it that we converse with God through Christ. Christ is the ladder, but it is faith that carries us up and down on this ladder. It is faith that makes the things of heaven real to the soul: *Faith is the substance of things hoped for, the evidence of things not seen* (Hebrews 11:1). By faith, these things become substance and real. Heaven becomes more real than earth. By faith, we learn to walk by faith, not by sight. Then we will be above the world in heaven, and as the fruit of your faith, wait for the appearing of Jesus Christ.

Paul wrote: *Our conversation is in heaven; from whence also we look for the Savior, the Lord Jesus Christ* (Philippians 3:20). Where a person's hopes and expectations are is where his life is. Christians expect Christ's appearing, so their life is fixed in heaven. Paul was saying this is not just a motion we go through. When we speak of conversing in heaven, we are not just pleasing our imaginations. By faith, we look on heaven as the most real thing in the world. We expect the Lord Jesus Christ before long to bodily appear in glory, and we will see Him with these eyes. He will change our vile bodies and make them like His glorious body. By faith, we look on these things to be real and close at hand. Waiting for these things is what puts our conversation in heaven. Our hearts are there because we expect these things will be made good to us quickly.

O Christians! Exercise your faith in Jesus Christ and produce the fruit of faith in waiting for the appearing of Jesus Christ when He shall come and appear in His glory. This will help make your conversations in heaven. What a blessed time that will be when Jesus Christ will come from the heavens and appear to those who have been waiting for Him! It was a blessed thing to have Christ here personally, even in His humiliation, and to live with Him when He was on the earth. How blessed will it be when He comes in His glory and changes our vile bodies to be like His glorious body!

> **He will change our vile bodies and make them like His glorious body.**

Oh, this will keep the heart in expectation of Christ, for that vile body of yours that is now a body of sin, death, disease, weakness – just a lump of clay – will be made like the glorious body of Jesus Christ. It will shine more gloriously than the sun in the sky. This will be when Jesus Christ will come with all His angels in His glory.

We will see this. When all the glory of the creature will be darkened with the glory of God and Jesus Christ, the bodies of the saints will shine gloriously before the face of God and Jesus Christ. They will be more glorious than the glory of the sun, for it will be darkened at the coming of Jesus Christ. The great glory of the Father, Jesus Christ, and the angels will darken the glory of the sun, moon, and stars, but the glory of the bodies of the saints will shine with such brightness that all the glory of God, Jesus Christ, and the angels will not darken their glory. If the glory of God and the angels should darken it, then to what purpose is it that their bodies will be like the glorious body of Jesus Christ?

But it will not darken their glory. Even though they will be put into the midst of the glory of God and His Son, their very bodies will shine in beauty and brightness there. If we believed this and waited expectantly for it every day, how it would change us!

I have a diseased and clumsy body, and it hinders me in every duty of worship and service. Wandering and vain thoughts lodge in me now, but I wait for that time when Christ will come in all His glory and make my body like His glorious one. He will make it able to look on the face of God and to be able to be employed in holy duties for all eternity without any weariness and without any intermission. The bodies of the saints will be raised strong, and their souls will be exercised about the highest things possible for a creature to be exercised with without weariness. This is what we wait for.

Many things here trouble my mind and spirit and hinder me in my fellowship with heaven, but soon the time will come when I will be delivered from all troubles here, when Christ will appear with His mighty angels to be admired by His saints. When He comes, He will take the saints and set them on thrones to judge the world. The expectation of this time will raise the heart to heaven.

But when I consider the glory that will be upon my soul, I think: "If this weak, fleshly body of mine will be raised to be more glorious than the sun in the sky by the almighty power of God whereby He is able to subdue all things unto Himself, then what height of glory will my soul be raised to? But not only my soul but also my grace, the divine nature that is in my soul, will be raised too.

The plants are capable of being raised to a higher excellency than stones; the rational creature to a higher excellency than a sensitive creature; the sensitive creature higher than the vegetative; and the supernatural creature to a higher excellency than the natural. So consider this: My body will be raised so high, what will my soul be then? And what will my graces that are in my soul be?

Oh, wait for this! In just a little while, I will be with God. He will be all in all to my soul, and I will enjoy full communion with Him. Exercise faith, and wait for it. Look for it every day. Every moment it is nearer and nearer. Your salvation is nearer than when you first believed. God has a little work for you here, but as soon as this is done, I will see my Savior. My soul will soon be with Him and enjoy full communion with Him in glory. My body will be raised to live forever with Him. I will be where He is and will enjoy all that He has purchased by His blood. I am capable of as much glory as the blood of Christ is worth.

> Your salvation is nearer than when you first believed.

The text says, It will be an eternal weight of glory (2 Corinthians 4:17). Here, I am not equipped to bear a weight of glory. If the glory of heaven would shine on me as much as it could, it would soon swallow me up. When the glory of God appeared to Daniel, he said, *And I Daniel fainted, and was sick certain days* (Daniel 8:27). If God would open the heavens and shoot some light from heaven into us, we too, would faint, be sick, and even die. God said, *There shall no man see me, and live* (Exodus 33:20). No one here can enjoy what God has prepared for His saints in heaven and live.

Therefore, let us be content for a while to be as we are and exercise our faith and hope in what will be. Then we will be able to bear the weight of glory and be able to stand before the face of God continually to enjoy those things that eye has not seen, nor ear heard, nor can enter into the heart of man to conceive

(1 Corinthians 2:9). Even though a man has a spiritual eye, a spiritual ear, and a spiritual heart enlarged to supernatural things, the things God has prepared for us are not only beyond the eye of sense but also the eye of reason. The eye of faith has not seen them fully, nor ear ever heard of them, nor mind conceived them.

These are the "clusters of Canaan" that we taste now – foretastes of the land of glorious rest for God's people. Now by the exercise of your faith and hope, live on these things every day. It would be an immense help to keeping your conversation in heaven. Where should our hearts and thoughts, where should our lives and conversations be, but where we expect such things as these are to be revealed very soon on the appointed day of Jesus Christ.

Walking With God

And *Enoch* walked with God: and he was not;
for God took him.
– Genesis 5:24

Chapter 1

Opening the Text

Genesis 5 records for us the genealogies from Adam to Noah. It is worth noticing how the record moves along quickly: Adam lived so many years and had sons and daughters and then died. The same pattern follows with each generation – until we come to Enoch, and God seems to stop. Instead of only noting how long he lived and his children, he added: *Enoch walked with God.*

The Holy Spirit gives three verses to Enoch. He tells how long Enoch lived before he begat Methuselah and that he walked with God. He gives us Enoch's total time on earth and then again mentions that he walked with God. It was as though the Lord said, "I cannot pass over My servant Enoch so quickly. He was a holy man in his generation. He was My delight – he walked with Me." Enoch walked with God.

Enoch was not only a man of holiness, but he was also a prophet. He conversed much with God, and God revealed much of His mind to him. The Holy Spirit mentions Enoch again in Jude: *And Enoch also, the seventh from Adam, prophesied of these, saying, Behold, the Lord cometh with ten thousands of his saints* (Jude 14). But where do we find *Enoch*'s prophecy in the

Bible? We have the prophecies of Isaiah, Jeremiah, and other prophets, but where is the prophecy of Enoch?

The Holy Spirit said that Enoch prophesied: *Behold, the Lord cometh with ten thousands of his saints.* We do not have a record of this prophecy recorded fully in words, but we do have a glimpse of his prophecy earlier in the text hidden in the name of his son, Methuselah. The name means, "When he dies, it will be sent." The name of Enoch's son meant something significant. When he died, there would be a sending out, that is, the flood. When he dies, it will come – a prophecy pointing to the coming of the flood. Enoch prophesied hundreds of years before the flood that it was coming. Indeed, Methuselah's death coincided with the year of the flood itself.

It is also striking that Methuselah lived longer than anyone else: *All the days of Methuselah were nine hundred sixty and nine years* (Genesis 5:27). Why so long? Perhaps God, in His mercy, was extending the time before judgment so that He might fulfil the prophecies of Enoch, yet the flood would come in God's appointed time. Enoch prophesied that the flood would come when Methuselah died, so because God had work to bring about and to defer the flood for a while after, Methuselah lived a long time.

God does lengthen or shorten men's lives according to the work He is doing, according to His purposes and what He intends to accomplish through them.

Now what does it mean that *Enoch walked with God*? Sometimes the word is used of a special service before the Lord, such as the priests: *Wherefore the Lord God of Israel saith, I said indeed that thy house, and the house of thy father, should walk before me for ever* (1 Samuel 2:30). Later in the same chapter, God said: *I will raise me up a faithful priest, that shall do according to that which is in mine heart and in my mind: and I will build him a sure house; and he shall walk before mine anointed for ever* (1 Samuel 2:35). So, walking with God is sometimes used for a special and holy service.

It is true that Enoch was a prophet, and he might be said to walk with God in regard of the special ministration of his prophetical office, but here, it is broader. It refers to a life of righteousness and holiness. Noah, Enoch's great-grandson, is also said to have walked with God: *These are the generations of Noah: Noah was a just man and perfect in his generations, and Noah walked with God* (Genesis 6:9). Noah, no doubt, was motivated by hearing of his great-grandfather's walk with God to walk in the same way.

Noah's walking with God is described as being righteous and in being blameless (Genesis 6:9). The Septuagint translates the phrase "walked with God" as "he pleased God." The writer of Hebrews uses this phrase when describing Enoch's faith: *By faith Enoch was translated that he should not see death; and was not found, because God had translated him: for before his translation he had this testimony, that he pleased God* (Hebrews 11:5). That word that you have here in Genesis is rendered, *he walked with God,* and in Hebrews, it is that he had this testimony, that *he pleased God*. Indeed, it is the same, for he walked in the ways that God was pleased and delighted in.

> Noah's walking with God is described as being righteous and in being blameless.

Some interpreters have suggested that Enoch only began walking with God after the birth of Methuselah since the text specifically notes it afterward. Some now think that Enoch was a wicked man before the time that he begat Methuselah. In that sixty-five year time, there is no mention of his walking with God: *Enoch lived sixty and five years, and begat Methuselah: and Enoch walked with God after he begat Methuselah*. But that is not sufficient ground to conclude that he did not walk with God before because it said he did do it *after*. Instead, it may emphasize the constancy of his walk with God – that from that point forward and throughout his life, he continued steadfastly in close fellowship with God.

So, that is all I need to say. The great doctrine we learn here is this: To walk with God is to live in continual fellowship with Him, in righteousness, and in ways that please His heart.

Chapter 2

The Excellence of a Christian Life: Walking with God

It is the great excellency and highest commendation of a godly man to walk with God. It is the highest testimony that can be given of anyone in this world. Notice that God emphasizes this. In Genesis 5, it is said twice of Enoch. Verse 22 says, *And Enoch walked with God* and again in verse 24, *And Enoch walked with God*. It is as if He loved to mention His poor creatures walking with Him. As though God delighted to repeat it: "This is what brings delight to my soul."

The same is true in the testimony of Noah. Perhaps in reading it, you have not noticed what I now draw to your attention: *Noah was a just man and perfect in his generations, and Noah walked with God* (Genesis 6:9). God did not say, "Noah was a just man and walked with God." Instead, He repeats Noah: *Noah was a just man and perfect in his generations, and Noah walked with God.*

It was as if He were saying, "Here is the blessed man who, though surrounded by a sinful and wicked generation, still kept close to Me. Yes, Noah was just and perfect – and Noah walked with God. Oh, I take delight in this Noah! Consider my servant Noah: Noah was thus, and Noah walked with God." The repeating of his name adds emphasis, for the sentence would make sense without it; but it is repeated for the sake of praise.

Noah was a just man and perfect in his generations, and Noah walked with God. Oh! What an excellency it is for a man to walk with God, and for God Himself to claim that man and say, "This man walks with Me." Men may practice the outward duties of religion yet still be strangers to God, never truly knowing what it is to walk with Him.

They may walk in paths of their own making while appearing to walk in God's way. As the stars are carried one way by the motion of the heavens, yet each has its own movement as well – so many, in their outward profession seem to move one way, but secretly, their hearts turn another way. The whole time they were praying, reading the Scriptures, listening to sermons, and claiming Christ, they were not walking with God. They made it look like it on the outside, but their hearts were not in it.

It is like a ship bound for one port, its sails set eastward, while a man walking on the deck may move westward. So too, one may seem to be sailing toward heaven in outward practice, while his private walk may be in another direction, to his own ends, his own designs.

But here is the honor of a man: when God Himself observes and owns him. As if God said of Enoch, "I see and search the hearts of all, and I have observed my servant Enoch. Not only in his outward profession of godliness, but in the secret of his soul, he walks with Me. He keeps no by-paths, no divided ways, but stays close with Me and walks with Me continually. Enoch walked with God."

This phrase, *walking with God,* is expressed in Scripture under several forms, all having the same purpose:

- Walking **before** God: Abraham said, *The* LORD, *before whom I walk* (Genesis 24:40), and God told

Abraham, *Walk before me, and be thou perfect* (Genesis 17:1). The psalmist wrote: *I will walk before the Lord in the land of the living* (Psalm 116:9), and Hezekiah asked the Lord to *remember now how I have walked before thee* (2 Kings 20:3).

- Walking **after** God: *Ye shall walk after the Lord your God* (Deuteronomy 13:4), like a child walking after his father yet truly walking with him.

- Walking **in the name of the Lord**: *We will walk in the name of the Lord our God* (Micah 4:5).

- Walking **in the Spirit** of God: *Walk in the Spirit* (Galatians 5:16).

Walking before God, after God, in the name of God, in the Spirit of God, and walking with God – they all come to the same purpose.

Now, to explain this further, I intend to look at it under four main points:

1. To explain what it means to walk with God – what work of God brings the soul into this walk and to describe in what way the soul walks with Him.

2. To show the excellency of this walk – what a blessed thing it is for a Christian to walk with God.

3. To give evidences – how you may discern whether a man truly walks with God.

4. To lay down some rules – how you may come to walk with God, how you may come to live so as to have this testimony, even from God Himself, that you walk with Him.

Chapter 3

How the Soul Is Brought to Walk with God

First, everyone by nature goes astray from God. The psalmist said: *The wicked are estranged from the womb: they go astray as soon as they be born, speaking lies* (Psalm 58:3). This is one of the earliest evidences of sin in children: From the very womb they go astray. It is natural to them, as soon as they have a being, to depart from God. The natural path of man is the way of death. It is the way of their own hearts, their own counsels. It is the common course of the world, the walk of the flesh.

But now the work of God in bringing the soul to walk with Him begins here:

A Stop in the Way of Sin

When God begins His saving work, the soul is first stopped in its natural course. Many are left to walk for a time in their natural way, the path of death, but at last God stops them by some mighty work of His Spirit. Then the soul begins to ask: "Where am I? What path is this? Where am I going? Can this be the way for an immortal soul? Is the way I am walking in likely to end well?" Fear usually rises – fear of eternal ruin. So then that soul concludes that it must go no further in the direction it had been going. No matter how pleasant the path is, how pleasing to the flesh, it would be foolish to keep on that way. So, God causes a stop.

The Way of Life Revealed

The Lord then sets before the soul the way of salvation, the way of life. It is as we read of Saul, when he was hurrying on in the way of death, a light shone around him and caused him to stop so that he could go no further. The Lord showed him the way of life. Isaiah said: *And thine ears shall hear a word behind thee, saying, This is the way, walk ye in it* (Isaiah 30:21). Oh! So many know this by experience. They have been walking in the ways of death, of eternal misery, and have blessed themselves in those ways. But there was a time when God caused them to hear a voice as it were behind them saying, "This is the way; walk in it. You are out of the way, but here is the way of life. If you do not want to perish eternally, walk in this way."

It is a secret voice that the Lord causes to be heard in the soul, but it is a powerful voice. Perhaps you have come to the Word and have heard what the way of life is, but it never turned your heart. But when God wants the soul to come walk with Him, He causes the soul to hear. Besides the outward voice of the Word, the Spirit speaks within, saying, "This is the way. You poor soul! You are wandering from the way of life and are on the way of eternal death. Come in, come in, here is another way. This is the way; walk in it." The Lord's voice causes a mighty change of course for the soul.

Reconciliation with God

Then the Lord makes peace with the sinner. He reveals the doctrine of reconciliation. For when the sinner is first enlightened, when he comes to know himself and God, the sight of God cannot help but be dreadful to a sinner who formerly walked in the ways of death. He knows his path is dangerous and there is a better way, but he is frightened by God. How can two walk together who are not at peace? *Can two walk together, except they be agreed?* (Amos 3:3).

There is naturally an enmity between Man and God. Every person in the world is naturally an enemy to God, and no one can walk with Him until reconciled. If you are walking in enmity with God, you are a stranger to this way of walking with God. No soul can say he has walked with God unless he has been reconciled to Him. God reveals this to the soul in some measure before it is able to walk with Him. This is what happened to Enoch, and he certainly came to walk with God by this. In Hebrews 11, the Holy Spirit said that Enoch walked with God by faith. *Without faith it is impossible to please him* (Hebrews 11:6).

> **If you are walking in enmity with God, you are a stranger to this way of walking with God.**

Without faith it is impossible to walk with God; therefore, there must be a work of faith to bring the soul to be reconciled so that there is agreement between the soul and God. Reconciliation must come first – and only by faith.

Fellowship beyond Peace

Yet even after the peace is made and God is no longer an enemy to the soul, there may be some distance. David and Absalom made peace. They were reconciled, but for a time, David would not see his son's face. There was not the familiar fellowship that would be expected between father and child. In the same way, the soul may know God is no longer an enemy but still not enjoy nearness with Him.

So even though peace has been made, a further work of God is required for the soul to walk with Him. God must manifest Himself in sweetness, love, mercy, and delight to the soul so that there may be a familiarity between the soul and God. It is one thing for me to know God is not an enemy and will not condemn me; it is another to understand and appreciate the sweet embrace of His mercy and the delight of His countenance and to know that He wants to deal with us as a friend does with his friend.

The Lord is pleased to manifest Himself to the soul in the sweetness of His love and delight. "Not only will you not be damned but will be eternally saved – you are the soul that My soul delights in. You are one that I take as My friend and that I love to deal with in sweetness and familiarity."

This is what is manifested to the soul to enable it to walk with God in the way that the Holy Spirit spoke of Enoch walking with God.

Guidance by the Spirit

God also sends His Spirit to guide the soul. *For as many as are led by the Spirit of God, they are the sons of God* (Romans 8:14). As a father takes his child by the hand and leads him along, so when a person comes to be a child of God, God puts out His hand and leads him so that they walk together. You have probably seen a father and child walking somewhere. The father puts out his finger, and the child takes hold of it and walks along with him. So the Lord puts His Spirit into a gracious soul, and God and the soul walk together, being led by the Spirit of God.

Isaiah records what the Lord says of the way of the redeemed ones: *And an highway shall be there, and a way, and it shall be called The way of holiness; the unclean shall not pass over it; but it shall be for those: the wayfaring men, though fools, shall not err therein. No lion shall be there, nor any ravenous beast shall go up thereon, it shall not be found there; but the redeemed shall walk there* (Isaiah 35:8-9). Though weak and foolish, they do not wander because the Spirit is their guide and keeper.

That is the privilege of the redeemed ones. This way of the Israelites walking from their captivity to the land of Canaan is a type of the walk of the soul with the Lord.

Brought to the Father by the Son

Finally, Christ Himself, the Son of God, takes the soul and brings it to the Father. As the Spirit leads, so the Son presents us to God. The Lord Jesus Christ brings the soul to the Father to bring God and the soul into familiarity. *Through him we both have access by one Spirit unto the Father* (Ephesians 2:18). We have access through Him. He takes us by the hand and brings us to the Father. We have access through Jesus Christ.

It is as though a prince takes a reconciled and pardoned traitor to his father. He takes him by the hand and says, "Come, I will bring you to my father. I will walk along with you to Him."

So it is with Christ. No sinner can ever walk with God unless Christ walks with him. When Christ walks along with him, God is no longer terrible, but He is made even sweeter, more amiable, and lovely. Why? Because Christ has him by the hand. God the Father has him in one hand, and Christ has him by the other. The soul walks in this blessed walk between the hands of God the Father and the Son, while the Holy Spirit leads and guides along the way.

Chapter 4

What It Means to Walk with God

When the soul is brought to God by Christ and enabled to walk with Him, what does the process of walking with God actually look like?

Walking with God Means Keeping the Eye on God

When the soul is enabled to walk with God, the first mark is this: It sets its eye continually on God.

Enoch walked with God: That is, Enoch, in the ways of his life, set God before him, and kept his eye on God. Those, like Enoch, who are walking with God:

- See the infinite beauty there is in God
- Acknowledge Him as the fountain of all good
- Understand that God is infinitely worthy of all honor and service

These three things cause the eye to be upon God continually, and a soul walking with God sees Him in this way all the time. *For thy lovingkindness is before mine eyes: and I have walked in thy truth* (Psalm 26:3). "Oh Lord! I see You as amiable, lovely, gracious, and the fountain of all good. Lord, I have walked in Your truth, setting God before me." *I have set the LORD always before me: because he is at my right hand, I shall not be moved* (Psalm 16:8).

A soul who walks with God scarcely sees anything but God. Even when enjoying created things, his eye is on God. As the little child walking with his father looks up to him, so every soul who walks with God has his eye on Him, for there is nothing as lovely to draw the soul to God as God Himself.

Wicked men do not find God to be such a lovely object. They do not see the excellence of Him, so they turn their eyes away: They *have not set thee before them* (Psalm 86:14). Those who walk according to the lusts of their own hearts in their wicked, sinful ways, do not have God in their thoughts: *The wicked, through the pride of his countenance, will not seek after God: God is not in all his thoughts* (Psalm 10:4).

The soul who walks with God looks for Him and sees Him before him.

Walking with God Means Living as in His Presence

The second mark is that the soul behaves itself as one who is in God's presence. I see myself in God's presence, and my eye is upon God, so now let me look to myself and make sure that the conduct of my soul is as one who is in the presence of so holy, so great, so glorious and blessed a God as the Lord is.

Paul said, *As of God, in the sight of God speak we in Christ* (2 Corinthians 2:17). When we do anything, we do it as of God, in the sight of God, knowing that we are always before God. Augustine said of Noah: "He walked with God, that is, he had God always present before his eyes, walking so holily, and so reverenced Him." This is to walk in the fear of God. This is the walk you will find the saints of God in all day long.

That is how you can recognize a saint of God – he will be walking in the fear of the Lord all day long. We are not to fear the Lord occasionally, but to *be thou in the fear of the* LORD *all the day long* (Proverbs 23:17). The walk of a Christian should be to order every action, from morning to night, to walk in the fear of the Lord; and nothing in this world or any temptation should be able to put him out of this walk. The Christian walking with God will work to behave himself as becomes one who stands in the presence of God.

Walking with God Means Following the Will of God

To walk with God is to walk in the same way He goes and doing what He does. God's way is holiness and righteousness. The soul that is ruled by the will of God will not be acted on by his own will. Whatever God will, I will the same thing. When the soul suits itself with God and sets the Lord as an example before it, then the soul walks the way God walks.

> To walk with God is to walk in the same way He goes and doing what He does.

The Scripture commands: *Be ye holy; for I am holy* (1 Peter 1:16). I see the holy and the righteous ways of God, and I labor as a dear child to follow Him. In all my affairs, I will work to resemble God Himself. This is to walk with God – to imitate Him.

Walking with God Means Seeking God's Glory

Walking with God is not only following His will but also having the same goals and ends that He does. What is the end of all of God's ways? It is that His blessed name is magnified and His glory proclaimed. So the soul that walks with God takes up this same design: "I will aim for the glory and honor of God, and every other thing will be subordinate to that." Just as two companions are said to walk together when they are bound for the same destination, so the saint walks with God by aiming for the same end – the honor of God's name.

We will come back to this later, but just the introduction to it shows its excellence. As you go along, examine your own hearts to make certain you are not strangers to God. Has God brought you to walk with Him? Do you keep your eyes on Him? Do you behave as if in His presence? Is the will of God the will of your soul? And is your ultimate goal the same as God's?

Walking with God Means Submitting to the Way He Works in the World

The person walking with God carefully observes the different ways in which He works in the world and then brings himself into alignment with them. God sometimes seems to work in one way, sometimes in another way. At times, He works in ways of judgment, sending heavy and dreadful afflictions – sometimes against His own saints. At other times, He shows Himself in ways of mercy. The soul that truly walks with God watches closely for these different administrations and says within itself, "Let me shape my heart to fit the Lord's ways."

If God is dealing in judgment, the soul replies, "Oh Lord! We will wait upon You in the way of Your judgments" (Isaiah 26:8), as God's people will one day sing in the land of Judah. When under affliction, it seeks to honor God there by exercising the graces that fit such a season. But if God is working in mercy, the soul suits itself accordingly and labors to bring out and exercise the graces that are suitable to those ways.

So too, in our personal lives: Whether God brings affliction into the family or mercy and prosperity, the person who is walking with God will work to exercise those graces that are suitable to His ways. Just as when we walk beside a man – if he turns one way, we turn with him; if he goes another way, we follow – so the soul that walks with God adjusts itself to all His various ways.

This is a great art and a deep mystery: to bring the soul into agreement with God's dealings in every condition. If God is dealing out mercy, there are some who can bless and praise God and think that they are walking with God. But if God turns His back on them and takes away their choicest earthly comfort, perhaps even your husband, wife, or dear friend, how will they walk then?

True walking with God means that when His way is mercy, we answer with joy, thanksgiving, and blessing His name; but when His way is affliction, we answer with faith in God, patience, and Christian wisdom, seeking to know what good I can get out of this hand of God. No matter what course God decides on, we have been given the graces we need to respond appropriately. Whether God leads through smooth paths or rugged ones, walking with God means we suit our soul to His and submit to His will.

Walking with God Means to Live in Holy Dependence on Him

To walk with God is to live in holy dependence on Him in all things. This dependence shows itself in four ways:

1. For Direction *Lead me in thy truth* (Psalm 25:5). The godly soul looks up to God and cries, "Lord, teach me Your way. Lead me in the path everlasting. Send out Your light and truth to guide me." He looks for God's guidance throughout his life and even into death.

Can you say that you walk in holy dependence on God for guidance and direction in every step? Whatever you do in your business or personal life, depend on God for direction. The more important the task, the more intensely should the heart seek after God for guidance.

But the men of the world are afraid that God will lead them into hard and troublesome paths, so they are wary of God's guidance. Wicked hearts will not trust God for His direction, but gracious hearts say, "Let God lead me where He will; it is enough that He goes before Me." The wicked are guided by their own thoughts, by their own counsel, by the examples of other men, and what is most suitable to their own ends, but the way of the saints is this: "Lord, guide me."

2. For Protection When a child walks with his father and hears a frightening sound, he looks up and relies on him for protection. In the same way, the believer, walking in God's way, expects to meet troubles and opposition, but he looks up for divine protection. We walk with God, depending on Him for safekeeping. "Lord, I am in the path that You have guided me to. Whatever trouble and affliction are on this way, protect and defend me in this way of Yours."

3. For Assistance The soul that walks with God depends on Him for strength in anything it undertakes. "Lord, this is the work that You have called me to. Grant me strength and assistance in this work. I can do nothing without You."

The wicked trust in the flesh and their own strength; therefore, the Lord has cursed them: *Cursed be the man that trusteth in man, and maketh flesh his arm* (Jeremiah 17:5). Occasionally, they may say they need God, but they are strangers to a holy, gracious frame of spirit that walks in a holy dependence on God for assistance with every part of their lives.

4. For a Blessing Last, the soul depends on God for blessing, success, and reward. The Lord said to Abraham: *Walk before me, and be thou perfect; I am thy shield, and thy exceeding great reward* (Genesis 15:1; 17:1). The godly soul, though it has little encouragement from the world to do so, looks up to God for His blessing. No matter how things go, he knows God will bring everything to good. That is a soul who is walking with God.

Walking with God Means Freedom and Readiness to Obey

One who walks with God in holiness and obedience finds his heart set free within him. He comes readily to every good work. He is not dragged or forced to God but walks with Him willingly. There is a vast difference between a prisoner being dragged along against his will and a friend who gladly walks beside you with delight and pleasure.

So it is not enough to simply be in the way God wants you to be or do the things God wants you to do unless your heart obeys freely and cheerfully. Walking with God means choosing the ways of holiness as the most suitable way for the soul.

David said, *I will walk at liberty: for I seek thy precepts* (Psalm 119:45). It is a notable Scripture. The world thinks liberty means satisfying their lusts without restraint. But David said that true liberty is found in seeking God's precepts. To the carnal heart, conformity and obedience to God's rule feels like the greatest bondage in the world; but to the gracious heart, God's commandments are liberty itself. In fact, accounting the precepts of God to be the greatest liberty to the soul is an excellent argument that grace is in a heart.

When we walk in sin, we are slaves of Satan, but when we walk in God's precepts, we are free. It is like a man strolling in the open fields compared with one locked in a dungeon. The soul that walks with God walks at liberty.

Walking with God Means Communion with Him in His Ordinances

An essential part of walking with God is the conversation and communion that the soul has with God in holy duties. These are the special walks of the soul with God, and of God, with the soul in the duties of holy worship. The Lord said, *Ye shall do my judgments, and keep mine ordinances, to walk therein: I am the* LORD *your God* (Leviticus 18:4). You must *walk* in God's ordinances. The ordinances of God are the *walks* of a gracious soul, and there the soul meets with God.

There is a notable Scripture that shows that God's ordinances are where the soul meets with Him: *And I will set my tabernacle among you: and my soul shall not abhor you. And I will walk among you, and will be your God, and ye shall be my people* (Leviticus 26:11-12). What did God mean when He said, *I will set my tabernacle among you*? He meant His ordinances. When you partake of His ordinances and engage in the duties of His worship, He will walk among you.

God walks among us when we enjoy His ordinances. In Leviticus 18, we see the ordinances are the godly man's walk; in Leviticus 26, the ordinances are God's walk. Both are walking the same way, and there God and a gracious heart meet together.

The churches enjoying ordinances are the candlesticks that we read of in Revelation 1:13: *In the midst of the seven candlesticks one like unto the Son of man, clothed with a garment down to the foot, and girt about the paps with a golden girdle.* The Lord Jesus Christ is in the midst of the candlesticks – that is, in the midst of the churches. Where the ordinances of God are, there He is, and if you want to walk with Him, you must look for Him there.

So David said, *They have seen thy goings, O God; even the goings of my God, my King, in the sanctuary* (Psalm 68:24). If you want to walk with another, you must know where he goes and where he walks. The sanctuary, in His ordinances, is where God is walking. If you want to walk with Him, you must find Him there.

The Song of Solomon tells us: *The king is held in the galleries* (Song of Solomon 7:5). Those galleries are His ordinances, the galleries of the great King of heaven and earth. Princes and other great men have sumptuous galleries that they use to walk in, and only their favorite people are allowed to be there to walk with them. The passage tells us that the king is *held* in the galleries; that is, when Jesus Christ is in communion with His saints in His ordinances in the duties of worship, it is as pleasant a gallery as He has in heaven itself. Oh! He loves to be there – the King is *held* there. Gracious hearts have much sweet communion in these galleries, these ordinances, walking with Jesus Christ.

When the soul is exercised in the ordinances, it communes with Christ. It listens to what Christ says, and Christ listens to the voice of the soul in return. *It is the voice of my beloved* (Song of Solomon 5:2). When they walk together in ordinances, Christ speaks to the soul, the soul knows His voice, and the soul speaks again to Jesus Christ. There is a blessed communion between them. Christ lets Himself into the heart, and the heart opens itself to Christ.

The communion that a gracious heart has with Jesus Christ in ordinances is unspeakable! Only those who are acquainted with it understand what the meaning of conversing with God there means. Many are like Adam who, when God came to walk in the garden, was hidden in the bushes. The ordinances and duties of worship are as Paradise, as Eden. God comes many times to walk with us and wants to have communion and conversation with us, but so many times we are hidden away, entangled in guilt or worldliness. Then, the presence of God is terrible to them, and the more the voice and presence of God is in an ordinance, the more they are afraid because of some guilt. They are caught in the bushes when they should be conversing with God.

This is a big difference between Christians. Some have such blessed words with God and sweet communion between God and their souls. But too many of God's children have some good in them but are entangled in the briars of the world. Though God is in the midst of His ordinances, they have no conversation, no communion with Him at all.

Walking with God is not a stagnant thing.

Walking with God Means Following Him More and More

Finally, walking with God is not a stagnant thing. As God reveals Himself more and more, the soul follows God more and more, seeking to glorify Him continually. Where there is true walking, there is progress in godliness.

When the soul is first led by the hand of Jesus Christ to God and comes to walk with Him, it is sweet and comfortable. But as God reveals Himself further to the soul, the soul grows still more holy, more gracious, honoring God more in its daily life, drawing nearer and nearer to heaven each day; this is to walk with God.

David described it this way: *My soul followeth hard after thee: thy right hand upholdeth me* (Psalm 63:8). Imagine a child walking with his father. The child, perhaps tired or weak, is having trouble keeping up with him, so the father puts out his hand and holds him. This so strengthens the child that he is now able to push on after his father. That is how it is here: O

Lord, Your right hand upholds me. If it did not uphold me, I could not walk. But You do hold me, so my soul follows hard after You, increasing more and more in godliness. In another place, David said, I will *praise thee more and more* (Psalm 71:14). Speaking of the honor that he desired to give to God, he professed he would still add to the praise of God and praise him more and more.

These, then, are the principal things that make up walking with God. Yet, one thing must be added, which runs through and completes them all: These are not occasional steps but the constant course of a man's life.

Some men, who do not know what it is to truly walk with God, may take a step or two in His ways. They may seem earnest for a time, but they quickly turn away, finding the path to be tedious and irritating to them. But the heart that truly walks with God does all these things – keeps his eye on God, lives as if in God's presence, walks where He walks, observes God's designs, and embraces obedience – and it does them in the daily course of life.

It is true, through the violence of some temptation there may be a stumble or even a fall. But the heart is still set on God. It gets up again, returns to God's way and carries on. Some carnal men may occasionally have their hearts touched while under God's hand of affliction or upon hearing a sermon and take a step onto God's path. But if you look at the constant course of their lives, it is in sin.

The difference can be seen in the swine that walks through a fair meadow. Though for a moment, it may walk among the grass and flowers, its heart is in the mire and dirt, and there it returns to wallow. So, it is with many wicked men – they may hear, pray, and do some good works, but their delight is in the lusts of the flesh, in sin, and it is there they remain and wallow. That is their proper place, and it is far from walking with God.

Or consider a beggar following a man for a little while, hoping to get something from him. But if the man keeps walking away, the beggar turns aside to something else and goes no further with him. So it is with many men, even many of those who profess to be Christians. They seem to follow God, hoping for comfort and blessing from Him, but if God does not give quickly what they are looking for, they turn aside and seek satisfaction elsewhere.

The difference between a friend walking with another out of delight of communion with him and a beggar who only goes along with a man hoping to get something from him is that the man begging for alms only cares about the man as long as he has any hope of alms from him. Once he gets what he wants or if he does not get it, he turns aside from the man. But what satisfies the person who is walking with his friend is the company of his friend and the conversation they will have as they walk along. So he goes with him steadily until they get to the place where his friend is going, even wishing the walk was longer so he could spend more time with his friend.

That is the difference between the false professors and the true saints. Perhaps some have a touch of conscience and see that if they do not have mercy from God, they will perish. They may seek God, follow God, and cry to Him for mercy. But if they do not receive the comfort they expect to receive, they turn away from God and seek comfort elsewhere. But a gracious heart, that is indeed turned to God, not only seeks God for mercy so it may be delivered from misery, but it sees the excellency of God and finds sweetness in communion with Him. He loves just being in His presence.

This love of God's presence is what gives constancy to the gracious heart in the ways of holiness. The soul that walks with God because of the communion and joy found with Him will hold out and endure to the end. One who merely serves God in a servile and self-seeking way will soon grow weary and turn away.

Think of a journey: If you have good company and especially good conversation along the way, you do not grow weary – the miles pass quickly. So it is with Christians. Because they have such blessed company in walking with God, the ways of God become sweet and easy to them, and thus they persevere.

Chapter 5

Twelve Blessings of Walking with God

There are many excellencies in walking with God:

1. Walking with God Makes His Ways Easy

What an excellency there is in walking with God! If it were only this – that it makes the ways of God easy – it would be worth a world. The soul who understands what walking with God means finds all the ways of God easy.

How grievous and sad is the condition of the men and women who, though convinced in their consciences and unwilling to forsake God's ways, find them heavy and tedious. They keep to them only out of necessity, not delight because they do not find communion with God in them.

But the saints find the ways of God easy because they walk in them with such good company. David said, *When I awake, I am still with thee* (Psalm 139:18). Even the nights are pleasant, for when he could not sleep, he still had the comfort of God's presence. Many cannot bear to lie alone. Those who cannot fall back asleep find the nights long and tedious when they have no one with them. *When I awake, I am still with thee.*

2. Walking with God Brings True Honor

This walking with God is not only sweet, but it is also most honorable. Attendance upon kings and princes is counted a great honor; even the maids of honor who attend a queen are esteemed highly. But how much greater honor is it not only to attend to a prince but also to freely converse with him. Or to walk as a friend with an emperor in his galleries, in his gardens, in his orchard.

So it is with the saints. Abraham was called *the Friend of God* (James 2:23). Christ Himself said, *I call you not servants, . . . but I have called you friends* (John 15:15). It is a great honor for God to allow the soul to come as a friend and to converse with Him as a companion.

The servants who stood in Solomon's presence were considered blessed – even more so who sat at his table (1 Kings 10:8). So what honor and blessing is it to be always with and walking with God! Even the angels' honor is that they behold the face of God (Matthew 18:10). So what an honor it is for Christians to be daily walking with God!

This is the honor and happiness of the church when she is in glory. Christ said it like this: *Thou hast a few names even in Sardis which have not defiled their garments; and they shall walk with me in white: for they are worthy* (Revelation 3:4). They will have glory put on them and will walk with Christ, for they are worthy. Walking with Christ is the greatest honor that Christ could promise them.

Again in Revelation, it is said of those who sang a new song, standing on Mount Zion with the Lamb: *These are they which were not defiled with women; for they are virgins. These are they* which follow the Lamb whithersoever he goeth. These were redeemed from among men, being the firstfruits unto God and to the Lamb (Revelation 14:4). They follow the Lamb wherever He goes – this is the honor given to them. Walking with God is most honorable.

3. Walking with God Satisfies the Soul

Another excellency of walking with God is the blessed satisfaction the soul enjoys in it. To walk with life itself, with glory, with happiness, and that in a constant way – must bring inconceivable satisfaction and peace to the soul.

Philip said, *Lord, show us the Father, and it sufficeth us* (John 14:8). If only to see God could satisfy, how much more to walk with Him continually! People will travel far just to catch sight of a great man; but to be admitted into the same room with him, to walk and talk with Him – this is far greater. God said to Moses, *My presence shall go with thee, and I will give thee rest* (Exodus 33:14). God promised Moses that His presence would be with him, and when the presence of God is with the soul, there is rest indeed. Joy floods the heart that walks with God.

> The soul on which the light of God shines never walks in darkness.

They shall be abundantly satisfied with the fatness of thy house; and thou shalt make them drink of the river of thy pleasures. For with thee is the fountain of life: in thy light shall we see light (Psalm 36:8-9). Certainly, where God walks, there is a glorious light all around. The soul on which the light of God shines never walks in darkness. The disciples who walked with Christ on the road to Emmaus said that their hearts burned within them (Luke 24:32), so must the hearts of the saints walking with God be filled with His influences and within them while they are walking with Him.

The psalmist wrote: *Blessed is the people that know the joyful sound: they shall walk, O* LORD, *in the light of thy countenance. In thy name shall they rejoice all the day: and in thy righteousness shall they be exalted* (Psalm 89:15-16). Those who walk with God walk in the light of His countenance, and in God's name, they will rejoice all day and be exalted in His righteousness!

No wonder saints have prized such communion above the treasures of the world. The Italian nobleman Galeazzo Caracciolo forsook all his honors and friends to move to Geneva to openly live his new Protestant faith. After experiencing sweet communion with God, he said, "All the silver and gold in the world is not worth one hour spent in the presence of Christ." A nephew of the pope, he had left much gold, silver, possessions, and family to go to Geneva to profess the truth there. He found it repaid in communion with Christ. One hour of walking with Christ is worth more than all the world. Ask the soul that has tasted this delight: Would you trade such an hour for ten thousand worlds? Oh, there is infinite sweetness in walking with God.

If communion with saints in prison could comfort a martyr like Dr. Taylor when he met the "Angel of God" John Bradford there, imagine the comfort to be found in communion with God Himself! A king once saw Plato walking up and down with other philosophers and cried, *"Oh, life! This is life and true happiness."* He recognized that all his kingdom could not afford him the happiness that he believed Plato and his fellow philosophers had conversing with one another. If that was true of philosophers walking together, then what life and happiness it must be for the soul to walk up and down with God!

Even in the valley of Baca (Psalm 84:6), even in the shadow of death and affliction, walking with God will be a walk of light and joy. It will sweeten your heart even in the midst of pain. Read where Jesus Christ leads the soul who walks with Him: *The Lamb which is in the midst of the throne shall feed them, and shall lead them unto living fountains of waters: and God shall wipe away all tears from their eyes* (Revelation 7:17). When you walk with Jesus Christ, He leads you to the living fountains of waters that comfort you. The comforts you had in the world were dirty puddles compared to these living streams. Here is an excellency beyond price – the abundance of soul-satisfaction found in walking with God.

4. Walking with God Is a Special Part of the Covenant

A further excellency is this: Walking with God is a special part of the covenant that God makes with us and is what much of the blessing of the covenant depends on. When God came to make a covenant with Abraham and to be a God to him and his seed, He required Abraham to: *Walk before me, and be thou perfect* (Genesis 17:1). God then promised to be the Almighty God and to be a God to him and his seed after him. As if that was all God looked at: Walk before me and be upright, and then you will have the blessing of the covenant.

We later see the same thing in the book of Micah. People asked: *Wherewith shall I come before the LORD, and bow myself before the high God? shall I come before him with burnt offerings, with calves of a year old? Will the LORD be pleased with thousands of rams, or with ten thousands of rivers of oil? shall I give my firstborn for my transgression, the fruit of my body for the sin of my soul?* (Micah 6:6-7). What do I do or what do I need to bring to please God?

The Lord's answer was plain: *He hath shewed thee, O man, what is good; and what doth the LORD require of thee, but to do justly, and to love mercy, and to walk humbly with thy God?* (Micah 6:8). "Do not bring Me occasional gifts or extravagant sacrifices. I want you to do justly, love mercy, and throughout your life, walk humbly with Me." That is what He prizes most.

This was Hezekiah's comfort when death was near. He turned

his face to the wall and prayed: *Remember now, O LORD, I beseech thee, how I have walked before thee in truth and with a perfect heart* (Isaiah 38:3). He was aware of his infirmities, yet he could appeal to the Lord: "Lord, I have walked before You in truth and with a perfect heart. Was that not what You required of my father Abraham? Lord, I have walked before You and been upright in some measure, so be Almighty God to me. Remember Your covenant and be a God to me because of this." And God heard him.

O my brothers! Is this not worth ten thousand worlds – that a soul may appeal to God and say, "Lord, I have walked with You"? Having kept the required part of the covenant on your part, you can be assured that God will faithfully fulfill His part of the covenant.

5. Walking with God Provides Safety

There is safety in walking with God. David, who walked much with God, said: *Though I walk through the valley of the shadow of death, I will fear no evil: for thou art with me; thy rod and thy staff they comfort me* (Psalm 23:4). I am walking with You, and though I am walking in the shadow of death, I will fear no evil. To walk with God is to walk in safety, even in the darkest valleys. *Though I walk in the midst of trouble, thou wilt revive me: thou shalt stretch forth thine hand against the wrath of mine enemies, and thy right hand shall save me* (Psalm 138:7).

Whatever the trouble may be, if God is with the soul, there is safety. *He that walketh uprightly walketh surely* (Proverbs 10:9), but it is said of the wicked that *he walketh upon a snare* (Job 18:8). The ways of sin and wickedness may seem pleasant and comfortable to you, but certainly you are on a snare, and you may be caught and undone forever. You may have escaped the trap so far, but you are in constant danger. Every step you take on the path of sin you are on top of a snare, in danger of falling to your eternal destruction.

But he who walks uprightly, walks safely with God. He says, "I know I am safe because I am with God." A child does not fear the road as long as he can see his father. So, the soul may know it is safe, no matter what danger comes, because it is walking with God.

6. Walking with God Brings Holy Boldness and Familiarity with Him

Walking with God also brings a holy confidence and familiarity with Him. At first, the majesty of God may fill the soul with fear and dread. But after the soul has conversed with God many times, holy confidence and familiarity grow. The soul learns to speak freely and has liberty to say anything to Him now.

Many who once knew nothing of the spirit of prayer nor of the liberty of pouring out the soul to God, after becoming acquainted with the ways of God and walking with Him awhile, find freedom in their spirits to open their hearts to God. It was said of Luther that when he prayed, he spoke to God as though speaking to a friend.

Acquaint now thyself with him, and be at peace (Job 22:21). What a phrase! The great God is willing to be our acquaintance. Poor men and women, servants and others, even poor godly people are often scorned by those around them. The rich and noble find it debasing to have any kind of acquaintance with those kinds of people. But the infinite God, even though He is so high that He humbles Himself to behold the things that are done even in heaven, is willing to be your acquaintance. The great people of this world are often praised when they humble themselves to converse with the lowly, but the high and holy God stoops to make the acquaintance of His people. Oh! Acquaint yourself with God. A familiarity with God and a holy boldness in His presence are blessings of walking with God.

7. Walking with God Reveals His Secrets

Another excellency is that walking with God brings us into the knowledge of His secrets. He who walks with God will come to know the mind of God. It is impossible for a man to take delight in walking with another without, in time, opening his mind to him. There is never any true friendship without a closeness of spirit. So it is in walking with God. The blessing of it is that such souls have the secrets of God revealed to them; they come to know much of His mind.

Though they are weak in their natural parts, they come to know much of God's mind because they are with Him. *He that walketh with wise men shall be wise* (Proverbs 13:20) – then what will he be who walks with God? Surely if there is wisdom to be learned from walking with wise men, then there is wisdom to be learned in walking with God. Even those with weak natural abilities often come to understand the mysteries of the gospel. Someone who just a while ago could understand nothing at all now comes to understand things beyond many great scholars.

How does this happen? He walks with the God of wisdom, and the God of wisdom delights to open Himself to him and to open His heart to him. They come to know the counsels of God because they walk with Him. Those Christians who keep close to God come to know more of the mind of God than others do. Others who walk loosely know little of the great mysteries of the gospel. They may speak of them, but they do not have spiritual insight into them. Those who walk with God, however, are entrusted with His secrets and learn to know His heart.

8. Walking with God Gains Favor in Prayer

The eighth benefit of walking with God is that such a soul finds favor in His eyes for the granting of petitions. *Delight thyself also in the* L*ord: and he shall give thee the desires of thine heart* (Psalm 37:4). If you are walking with God, enjoying conversation and communion, and delighting yourself in Him, He will give you what your heart desires. Just as if a man wants to petition a king or some great person, he looks for an opportunity to present it. He watches him to see when he might be heard and his petition accepted. I read of one man who offered a great sum of money to be able to whisper something in the king's ear each day. He did that because he thought many people would come to *him* for help with their petitions, and he would make back his money that way. The person who walks with God already has His ear. He has constant opportunity to present his petitions to God, and the Lord delights in hearing of them.

Now, there is a vast difference between the prayer of one who only formally professes Christ and the prayer of a truly godly person who walks with God. Formal professors may pray, but they are like beggars standing at your door, asking for alms. But those who walk with God are like a friend who needs a favor. You open the door for him and bring him into the best room of your house where he speaks freely as a friend. Both come to ask a favor from you, but one stays at the door, and the other has the privilege of coming into your home and speaking freely. One stands there and knocks but never sees God's face because He never opens the door for him. But a gracious heart that walks with God has the door opened for him when he knocks, and he is brought into the very presence of God who asks him what he needs. This is the privilege of those who are gracious and holy, who walk with God. They have freedom and privilege in prayer and the assurance that God will grant their petitions.

9. Walking with God Transforms with Glory

In walking with God, there is a glory that shines upon the soul. Moses went up the mountain and spent forty days with God. When he came down, his face shone so that the people were not able to look at him. God appeared in a visible manner to him, but spiritually, it is true now. Those who converse with God "forty days," consistently throughout their lives, have a beauty and luster, a glory put on them – so much so that those who have enlightened consciences but remain guilty are scarcely able to bear the sight of them.

I ask you, have you not felt it? When you have given in to some sin and then are around someone godly who walks closely with God, has it not struck terror into you? For there is a glory and beauty on those souls that walk closely with God. They shine in the midst of a crooked and perverse generation (Philippians 2:15). The glory of heaven is but the reflection of God's presence; so too, in measure, the Christian walking with God bears the glory of heaven even in this world.

10. Walking with God Draws Out Every Grace and Keeps Them Alive

Walking with God draws out every grace and puts them each into action. The graces of the Spirit of God are always kept in action. Just as fire kindles fire, the infinite holiness of God stirs up the holiness of those in His presence. The holiness in those walking with God will have the holiness in their hearts drawn out, enlarged, and exercised. A great blessing of walking with God is the continual drawing out and strengthening of every grace of the Spirit.

11. Walking with God Removes the Fear of His Presence

The soul that walks with God will never find His presence terrible, whether at death or at judgment. To the ungodly, death and the appearance of Christ in glory are dreadful, but those who now walk with God and converse with Him often, are not frightened by death. God's presence will not be terrible then. Even when Jesus Christ will come in flaming fire to revenge Himself upon those who do not know Him, the presence of Christ will not be terrible to them. Why not? Because they walked with Christ all the days of their lives.

They shall walk after the LORD: *he shall roar like a lion* (Hosea 11:10). Mark how these two are joined together: Wicked and ungodly men will tremble at the roaring of a lion, but it will not be frightening to the saints. And how much is it worth to have the terror of death and the final judgment taken away? Friends, the manner in which God appears at death and at times of judgment are different than in the times of prosperity. You may see no terror in God's presence now, but beware of it when death is approaching. The wicked find their deathbeds to be places of terror.

> The wicked find their deathbeds to be places of terror.

But those who walk with God will not find it so. When they come to die and God appears to them, they think these thoughts: Now I am going to stand before the great God to have my eternal estate determined one way or other. But what God is this? He is great indeed, but He is my friend. I have walked with Him all the days of my life. And when Jesus Christ comes to judge with thousands of His angels in glory, it is the same Christ I have conversed with all the way. Christ the Judge is Christ my friend. This removes the terror of death and judgment and fills the heart with peace. This will be the comfort in walking with God.

12. Walking with God Ends in Eternal Communion

Finally, it is the end of the walk that crowns it all. How blessed it will be! To walk with God now is sweet, but the end of the walk is eternal glory. No matter how many difficulties you may face in this life, if you come to enjoy God at last, you have reason to bless God. If you were going to possess a kingdom, though the way was exceedingly difficult and hard, it would be worth it because the destination was a kingdom. You who are walking with God, you have comfort in your walk now, but the end of your walk will be glorious indeed! You will possess a kingdom and have the crown of glory set upon your heads. The communion you have with God here is but a forerunner of the glorious communion you will enjoy with Him together with the saints and angels for all eternity.

And so, we have given you the chief excellencies of walking with God. It is no wonder, then, that the Holy Spirit gave such a high commendation to Enoch above all things – that he walked with God – seeing there is so much good in it. I had not thought to leave this subject without some further application. I wanted to press it on your hearts so that you might walk with God and not lose the comfort, blessing, and sweet excellency that I have described to you in walking with God.

Let me at least say this much: Be in love with it. Know that there is not true good in any other path. The devil deceives you, your own hearts betray you, and the world fools you if it promises any good that can compare with this. Walking with God is the Christian's true good, his happiness, his glory, his highest commendation. Oh, may this be recorded of you as it was of Enoch! *And Enoch walked with God.*

Chapter 6

Exhortations to Walk with God

Before we move on to the evidences of walking with God, I want to make a few applications of this exhortation to walk with God.

Bless God for His Willingness to Walk with Us

First, give thanks to God that He is pleased to walk so closely with His poor creatures. Praise Him for His great kindness! The angels are happy to stand before the Lord, but how much happier are we who are allowed such free fellowship with God! We who were once not only strangers but enemies of God are now welcome to walk with Him. What a blessed privilege it is!

Let us magnify the Lord for His goodness to us. He humbles Himself just *to behold the things that are in heaven* (Psalm 113:6), yet He stoops even further to walk with His poor, sinful creatures here on earth. Perhaps we could understand if we had been completely freed from sin, but God walks with us while we are still so low and sinful. If God only promised that one day we would see His face after a long, weary pilgrimage, that alone would be more than we deserve. But He grants us even now the privilege of fellowship with Him here, in this life. Blessed and magnified be His name!

Recognize the World's Strangeness to This Walk

Second, consider how utterly foreign this truth is to most of the world. To most people, walking with God is a riddle, an empty phrase. Scripture describes the walk of sinners in many ways: They walk after their own counsels (Psalm 81:12), after the flesh (Romans 8:1), after their lusts (2 Peter 3:3), after the course of this world (Ephesians 2:2), in the vanity of their minds (Ephesians 4:17), contrary to God (Leviticus 26:21), and according to men (1 Corinthians 3:3).

The Holy Spirit condemns not only walking according to the world and men, but He also condemns walking in the way of kings (2 Chronicles 28:2). If we were going to follow any man, we might think it was commendable to follow the king, but here, Ahaz was charged because he walked in the ways of the kings of Israel. In 2 Kings we are told that the kings themselves were walking in the ways of heathens (2 Kings 17:8).

We cannot even say that we can always walk according to the law because at times, the laws of the kings were evil. The kings' laws were in opposition to God's laws. Yet another passage talks about walking the wrong way: *He did evil in the sight of the Lord, and walked in the way of his father, and in his sin wherewith he made Israel to sin* (1 Kings 15:26). So God condemns walking in the way of great men, walking in the way of the laws of the places where we live, and walking according to our fathers.

Last, God condemns walking according to the common course of the world. Yet this is the walk of sinners. Scripture says that wicked men walk in darkness (1 John 1:6), after their own imaginations (Jeremiah 9:14), in the vanity of their minds

(Ephesians 4:17), in lies (Jeremiah 23:14), after the sight of their own eyes (Job 31:7), and after their covetousness (Ezekiel 33:31). There are almost twenty kinds of walks of sinners in the Scriptures. Those who walk in the way of sinners – in the vanity of their own minds according to the sight of their own eyes, after their covetousness, after the flesh, their lusts, and all the other kinds of descriptions – certainly, the end of their walk can be no other than destruction and eternal misery. The saints, by contrast, are called to walk with God.

Rebuke for Our Backward Hearts

Third, consider what vile hearts we have that are so slow and unwilling to walk with God when God graciously invites His saints to do so! Even the godly deserve rebuke for this. Walking with God is our glory. It is what makes our lives comfortable. It could turn this wilderness of ours into a paradise, our gardens into Edens, our houses into churches, and the church a heaven for us. Yet how backward we are!

> Consider what vile hearts we have that are so slow and unwilling to walk with God.

We need to consider this when we are in our walk and begin having vain thoughts. Think of your walks in gardens, your nice rooms or fields – how often are your thoughts vain, foolish, or even sinful? Who are you really conversing with? Are you not, many times, walking with the devil and making provision for the flesh? You should be walking with God. Are you really the saints of God? Is God offering Himself to walk with you, but you are walking with the flesh and conversing with the devil instead? Are your thoughts consumed by sin and wickedness? Oh, what a vile and sinful thing this is!

How shameful that saints should give sin God's place in their walk. You have walked with God – why do you not walk more closely? Do you excuse yourself by saying that business and worldly affairs keep you from fellowship with God? Yet when you have time off from the world and your obligations or you have time while walking from one place to another when you might commune with God, how little time you spend with Him! Truly, our hearts are backward from that which is our happiness and glory!

Exhortation to Walk Closely with God

Fourthly, let us be exhorted to keep close to God in our walk with Him. When Peter saw Christ walking on the water, he leaped out, even in the storm, to meet Him. Even if we have to go through afflictions to walk with Christ, it should be comfortable for us. We read in Scripture that idolaters would pass their children through the fire to get to their gods. Should we not endure difficulties to get to God? The Lord is willing to hear us and fellowship with us. He is ready to meet us word for word, promise for promise, embrace for embrace. If we would speak to Him, He would speak to us. If we would open our hearts to Him, He would open His heart to us. If we would promise to Him, He would promise to us.

The Lord often calls us to walk with Him. Think of the way dear friends will say to one another, "Come, let us walk out together." Though they may be busy, they will gladly stop what they are doing because their dear, loving friend has called them to walk.

Many times, God, our dear friend, calls us, "Come, let us walk out together." Any time that God darts a heavenly thought into your minds, He is calling you to walk with Him there. He wants you to follow that thought. The following of that heavenly thought darted into your minds is the answering of God's call to walk with Him. Do not ignore or turn away from those calls. In them lie great comfort, joy, and strength for your soul.

The Foretaste of Heaven

The fifth and last application I will make is this: If walking with God on earth is so excellent, imagine what it will be in heaven! If our fellowship with Him here is so sweet, how much sweeter will it be when we walk with Him in white, clothed with glory, with souls fit to converse with God. Now, we are very unfit to converse with the Lord because of our blindness and darkness. Our ignorance hinders us.

An unlearned man can gain little from conversing with a scholar because he is unable to ask good questions or understand what the scholar talks to him about, especially if it is deep and complicated. So, many who are very weak when they are in discourse with those that are strong and godly are not able to make as much use of that discourse as others can. It is a great excellency to be able to improve their ability to converse with people with greater abilities and strengths.

We are not able to draw out the fulness of God's fellowship here, but in heaven, we will be able to. We will know as we are known. We will understand God. If God communicates Himself, we will be able to receive every beam of His glory that He is pleased to let out. We will be able to walk with God and delight in His company without end.

Saint Bernard, of the gracious visitations of the Spirit of God to his soul said, "Sweet, if it were not so little." Even the best experiences of God's presence here are short and passing. But then it will be constant. We will then follow the Lamb wherever He goes and walk with Him in white according as He speaks. Now, the church cries out: "Oh, draw us, and we will run after You" (Song of Solomon 1:4). The Spirit of God needs to draw us here on earth, but then we will not need drawn. We will come on our own from the inclination of our own hearts. We will walk and converse continually with God – we will have nothing else to do.

I will walk in thy truth: unite my heart to fear thy name (Psalm 86:11). I find much sweetness and good in walking in Your truth here, O Lord. Unite my heart to the fear of Your name. Lord, keep me always here. It is good being here, as Peter said when Christ was transfigured in His glory. So, when the soul is walking with God, it says that it is good being here.

Well, when you are in heaven, you will always be with the Lord, just as the Scripture says. So, from the sweetness you find in walking with Him here, learn to long after heaven, where you will be continually in His presence. Only those who have truly tasted this joy on earth will fully grasp what I mean.

Think of it this way: Suppose all the blessed experiences you have ever had of God – the manifestations of His love, the stirring of His Spirit, the soul ravishing joys He has given you – were gathered together into one moment and you experienced them all again at this instant. What a comforting time that would be! Some have said, "Oh, the sweet communion I had with God! I would give the world to have it again!" Well, you had it once, but it was quickly gone. Then you had it a second and a third time; many times when you have been with God, He poured His grace into your soul and you want to experience it again. Well, imagine you had, in the next quarter of an hour, all the comfort and joy that ever you had in your life put all together – what a comforting quarter of an hour this would be!

Now in heaven, that joy will not be passing. For all eternity you will have that kind of communion with God, only infinitely greater, without end. What glory will heaven be!

If I were to describe heaven to a carnal man, I might speak of crowns of glory, glorious sights, freedom from sorrow, or a kingdom to inherit. But if I describe heaven to a saint, I will say this: You will have perfect communion with God. All those soul-ravishing comforts you have ever known in the presence of God in this world will be gathered up and multiplied beyond measure. This is the true excellency of heaven. This is what makes the saints long for it and prize it above all else.

Chapter 7

Marks of a True Walk with God

Having spoken of the excellency of walking with God, the natural question is: Who, then, are those who truly walk with Him? To answer this, I will set out ten evidences by which men and women may discern if they are indeed walking with God.

1. Walking by Faith, Not by Sight

The first evidence is this: Those who walk with God do not lean heavily on sense or reason in the course of their lives. They are not bound to judge all things by what they see or by what seems reasonable to them, for they have received a higher principle.

Most people in the world walk according to their senses, guided by what pleases the eye or the flesh. But the walk of one who walks with God lies beyond sense and above reason. He is not shaken when sense and reason appear to go against him. His heart remains calm, for he has something deeper that steadies him. As Paul said: *For we walk by faith, not by sight* (2 Corinthians 5:7). Beyond our sight – either beyond our sight of sense or the sight of reason – we walk by faith. The life of faith rises above sight and reason.

2. Being the Same in Public and in Private

A second evidence of walking with God is consistency: The believer is the same in secret as in the open. Whatever holiness and devotion appear outwardly before others, the same is found in his private life. He is the same man in public and private.

Why? Because he does not live merely before men but before God, so he seeks to honor Him in every place and in all his ways. David talked about how he lived at home: *I will behave myself wisely in a perfect way. O when wilt thou come unto me? I will walk within my house with a perfect heart* (Psalm 101:3). He would not walk with a perfect heart out in public only, but he also walked wisely when he was at home with his family.

Many seem strict abroad but are careless at home. You will find as much difference in the way men live in public and in private as you will in their clothes. Many men and women, when they leave their homes, will be very neat. Though they may have little means, they will spend what they do have on clothing so that they may look fine to the world. But if you were to go to their homes with their families, you would see that they do not care what clothes they wear there.

It is just so in regard of their lives: Their lives have as much difference as their clothes. When they are in public, they put a good face on things and seem to be very fair in their conversations and speak good things; but at home, they are forward and perverse, and perhaps in their anger, will swear. In their houses, they are profane and ungodly and vent their corruptions in a most ungodly manner.

Do you walk with God? If you do, you would be the same at home with your family as you are out in public with other people. Your wife, children, and employees could give as good a testimony of you as when you are out with others. And if you could go with those who walk with God into their place of private prayer, you would find them the same there as in any other duties of religion.

Many are pious out in public but dull and dead when they are at home with family or with God in prayer. Their own consciences tell them so. Those who walk with God will be as spiritual in the one as in the other. Perhaps when they are with others, because they are speaking on behalf of others when they pray in public, they may adjust their words or style to fit the group; but when they are alone and with their families, their hearts are as spiritual and as holy in their duties as when they are with others. Why? Because God is with them in both.

3. Having a Serious and Composed Spirit

Another evidence is a serious spirit. Walking with God will compose the spirits of men and women. It will remove lightness, vanity, and frivolity. Therefore, walking in the vanity of the mind is quite contrary to walking with God. Paul said, *Walk not as other Gentiles walk, in the vanity of their mind* (Ephesians 4:17). All wicked men walk in the vanity of their minds, but all those who walk with God walk in the seriousness of their minds.

It is necessary for them to have a seriousness of spirit in all their ways, for it is God they are dealing with. They cannot run this way and that as others do. If servants are walking with one another, they have the liberty to go out of their way to talk to a friend or anyone as they please. But if a servant is walking with his master or mistress, he dare not take that liberty but must walk where they walk. Many people who walk only with the creature, take liberty to run up and down as they please, but those who walk with God must have composed spirits and walk seriously.

Even though Christians walk seriously, they also walk cheerfully – for true Christian joy is always mingled with seriousness. Seneca, though a pagan, could say, "True joy is a serious thing." There is a kind of seriousness in true joy, for a Christian's joy is not superficial or frivolous; it is steady and composed. Even in rejoicing, a Christian shows seriousness.

First, a Christian's joy is disciplined. He is able to govern himself and call back even abundant joy at a moment's notice in order to engage in the most spiritual and solemn duties. His heart is never so carried away by earthly joys that he cannot call it in again. Certainly, you do not joy as a Christian if you cannot take your heart from earthly joys. God gives liberty to be merry, but the believer must be in control of his merriment, able to quiet his heart whenever duty calls.

Second, this kind of joy not only leaves him free to engage in holy duties, it actually makes him more fit for them. True and serious joy does not hinder devotion but prepares the soul for it. Christians must beware of foolishness, silliness, and vanity, for walking with God cannot help but make us serious. Those who are foolish and silly prove they do not truly converse with God, for God is such a serious object that fellowship with Him must impress a holy seriousness in the spirits of men.

4. Walking in Newness of Life

Those who walk with God do so in newness of life. It is not natural for us to walk with God; it is only possible after God mightily converts our spirits. It is natural for us to walk with our lusts and with the devil on our way to hell, but one who walks with God walks in newness of life: *As Christ was raised up from the dead by the glory of the Father, even so we also should walk in newness of life* (Romans 6:4). *Paul also wrote: And as many as walk according to this rule, peace be on them, and mercy* (Galatians 6:16).

You might ask, What rule did Paul mean here? I confess that ordinarily you would apply it to the walk according to the Scriptures. It is true that the Word of God should be the rule of our walk and our lives and that those who walk according to that rule will have peace. But I do not think that is the meaning of this text.

I think Paul intends for us to get the meaning from the previous verse: *In Christ Jesus neither circumcision availeth any thing, nor uncircumcision, but a new creature* (Galatians 6:15). *And as many as walk according to this rule*: that is, according to the rule of the new creature, not so much on outward things and duties like circumcision or uncircumcision but the walk of the new creature. And those who walk according to the rule of the new creature, those who behave like a new creation in their walk, *peace be on them.*

5. Passing through the Creature to God

Those who walk with God do not stop at created things but quickly pass through them to God. Those in this world who are acquainted with this mystery of godliness in walking with God must deal with the things of this world, but they do not linger there. They enjoy sweetness from the creatures as well as others, but after the encounter is over or even while still in the midst of it, their hearts rise beyond it to God Himself. Oh, there is so much sweetness in God! If the creature is sweet, so much more is God.

When those who walk with God enjoy the company of

friends, they think how much sweeter it is to have fellowship with Him. When they find comfort in a husband or wife, they are reminded of the deeper comfort they have in their true Husband, Jesus Christ. And when they have security and comfort in a peaceful home, they cannot help but think of the perfect rest they have in God, their eternal dwelling place.

Those who are of the world remain fixed on created things and do not know this way of walking with God. But believers, in all they enjoy, quickly turn through the creature to the Creator and rely on and rest in Him.

6. Loving Times of Retirement with God

Those who walk with God love to withdraw from this world. It is true, they must still follow their daily business in obedience to God, but unless they can have times of retirement, they hardly know how to live. Even in their calling, they strive to walk with God, keeping their hearts lifted toward heaven.

There is a great difference between walking with a friend in company with others and walking with that friend alone. So it is with the saints of God. While they must converse with the world and can find something of God even there, it is not the same as when their souls are alone with Him. That is where they find the sweetest and most comforting communion.

Therefore, they deliberately set aside times of retirement for meditation and prayer. Of Isaac we read: He *went out to meditate in the field* (Genesis 24:63), or to pray, for in Scripture, meditation and prayer are often joined as one. David could say that he poured forth his meditations, meaning his prayer (Psalm 142:2). So, because they should be joined together, Isaac went out into the field to meditate and to pray.

If those who walk with God live in a house with no private room, they will still find some time and place to be alone with

Him. Others, however, know nothing of this. When they are by themselves, their minds wander here and there, chasing every distraction like feathers in the wind. Solitude feels like a prison to them. They cannot imagine why men and women would willingly shut themselves away unless they are sick with melancholy.

O poor soul! You do not know what secret walks they have with God at those times. They are not alone. They would not trade their retired times with God for all your festivities, feasting, music, laughter, and endless talk. You may think you are living a brave life, but they would not exchange their sweetest solitary moments for the best of your merriment with your friends. For the one who walks with God values his hours of retirement as much as his busiest labors in the world.

> For the one who walks with God values his hours of retirement as much as his busiest labors in the world.

7. Keeping Even Accounts with God

Those who walk with God are careful to keep even accounts with Him. They daily ask themselves: "Is everything all right between my soul and God? Have I allowed anything to come between us?" For how *can two walk together, except they be agreed* (Amos 3:3)? So they are very careful to keep their agreement with God.

Indeed, Jesus Christ, the great Reconciler, first reconciled their souls to God so they are able to walk with Him. But believers must still, throughout their lives, keep up their agreement with God and keep short accounts with Him so that they do not become ensnared in the world and in the corruptions of their own hearts. That is what will happen to men and women who do not daily keep their accounts even. They will ensnare their souls in the world and in the lusts of their own hearts until God and their souls are strangers – until they are almost afraid to even think of God.

That is the reason many people are reluctant to pray and to come to the ordinances to commune with God. They have not kept their accounts even with God but have run in arrears with Him. Their hearts are entangled in the world and in their lusts, and now the presence of God is dreadful to them.

Oh, what a poor soul is a Christian who finds the presence of God grievous to him when it should make him glad: *I was glad when they said unto me, Let us go into the house of the LORD* (Psalm 122:1). If he does not keep his accounts even, his time alone is grievous. In fact, he tries to avoid being alone so he does not have to think about it.

But the soul that keeps even with God is able to rejoice when he can spend time alone with God or when he even thinks of God. That is a special part of walking with God. And I tell you, observe this rule. It is an evidence of walking with God and will help you walk with Him. Keep your accounts clear. You will then look forward to communion with God and rejoice to enter His presence.

8. Delighting in Spiritual Truths, Ordinances, and Fellowship

The more spiritual any truth, ordinance, or company is, the more the soul that walks with God delights in it. When one who is used to conversing with God meets a truth filled with God, he embraces that truth. When he partakes of an ordinance in which God shines, his heart rejoices. When he joins company where God is visible, he is filled with delight. A heart that converses with God says, "I have had sweet walks with God, and now I see the image of God reflected in these truths, ordinances, and people." The more spiritual they are, the more he delights in them.

By contrast, a carnal heart that walks according to the flesh and in the way of the world delights only if the truths have some kind of human reason or judgment in them. He will take delight if he finds wit, rhetoric, or eloquence. But he finds no delight in any spiritual truths – only in their outward human covering.

Those who are spiritual take delight in spiritual things. The more spiritual they are, the more delight they take. Ordinances are only dry meat to those who are carnal unless there is something external. If you bring the ordinances to them in the plain simplicity of the gospel, where there is only communion of saints sitting around a table eating a piece of bread and drinking a little wine, then they see no excellency there. But a gracious heart delights most when there is less of man and more of God.

9. Walking in All the Commandments of God, Blameless before Men

Those who walk with God endeavor to walk in all His commandments, righteous before God and blameless before men. It is written of Zacharias and Elisabeth: *They were both righteous before God, walking in all the commandments and ordinances of the Lord blameless* (Luke 1:6). They walked with God not in just one part of their lives but in all commandments and ordinances of God. Not only that, but they were also blameless before men.

Zacharias's chief job was to converse with God, but he was still careful to be blameless before men. He not only obeyed God in private, but he also lived in a way that men could not find fault. Being blameless before men concerns the honor of God.

Apply this to yourself: Can you truly say, "Lord, You know all things. You know there is no command or ordinance of Yours that my soul does not agree with. I desire to spend my life in them and to walk blamelessly before men"?

Many speak of walking with God, yet they walk carelessly

and negligently before others. If that is you, listen to what the Lord says to you today: Unless you walk blamelessly before both God and man, you do not know what it means to walk with God.

10. The Walk of the Saints Described in Scripture

Scripture describes the walk of the saints with God. I will look at several passages with you that describe the saints' walk with God.

Walking in Humility
God requires our walk to be one of humility. The heart that walks with God must be very humble in the presence of God. *He hath shewed thee, O man, what is good; and what doth the* LORD *require of thee, but to do justly, and to love mercy, and to walk humbly with thy God* (Micah 6:8). God wants that more than thousands of offerings and sacrifices.

    A proud man or woman never knows what it is to walk with God. Walking with God causes humility. Nothing so humbles the soul as communion with God. Pride and haughtiness in a person are proof that they converse little with God. When Job said to God: *I have heard of thee by the hearing of the ear: but now mine eye seeth thee*, he concluded by saying: *Wherefore I abhor myself, and repent in dust and ashes* (Job 42:5-6).

> Walking with God causes humility.

Walking in Uprightness and Truth
The Christian's walk is in uprightness: *Walk before me, and be thou perfect.* I could give you twenty passages for that, how uprightness is the walk of a Christian with God, but I will mention only one: *For I rejoiced greatly, when the brethren came*

and testified of the truth that is in thee, even as thou walkest in the truth (3 John 3).

The New Testament uses the words "walking in the truth" where the Old Testament talks about "walking in uprightness." This certainly references walking according to the truth of the gospel in the truth and sincerity of our hearts. *They testified of the truth that is in thee*, that is, the Word of the gospel prevailed in your heart, and since it did, you were able to walk in the strength and power of that truth and according to the truth. That is walking with God.

In verse 2 of this same chapter, John used a strange expression when he referred to Gaius: *I wish above all things that thou mayest prosper and be in health, even as thy soul prospereth*. It seems this Gaius had a poor, weak, sickly body but a very good soul. John said he wants him to prosper as his soul has prospered.

If we had as good a body as our soul, it would be a curse to many of us, but John could say that about Gaius. How did he come to have such a prosperous soul? He walked in the truth and according to the truth. All that he did was in the truth and sincerity of his heart. Even if we are weak in body, if we walk in the truth, our souls will prosper.

Walking in the Fear of God
Believer should always walk in the fear of God: *Also I said, It is not good that ye do: ought ye not to walk in the fear of our God because of the reproach of the heathen our enemies?* (Nehemiah 5:9). Walking with God and in the fear of God are closely related. And he gave the argument there, *because of the reproach of the heathen*. So, I say to all Christians who call themselves godly Christians, should you not walk in the fear of God? No matter how other people live their lives or what they follow, you are to walk in the fear of our God. The fear of God is continually on the walk of a Christian.

Look what we read of the early church: *Then had the churches rest throughout all Judaea and Galilee and Samaria, and were edified; and walking in the fear of the Lord, and in the comfort of the Holy Ghost, were multiplied* (Acts 9:31). It is an excellent Scripture. Do you desire to be built up in godliness? Then let the fear of God be on you.

Walking in the Joy of the Holy Spirit
You may object that fear will hinder our joy, but my answer is that the way to have true joy in the Holy Spirit is to walk in the fear of God. You may keep company with vain and wanton spirits who are always merry and full of mirth, yet they never allow any kind of seriousness – the kind we spoke of earlier. Their merriment is foolish, carnal, and shallow.

Those who have the deepest joy in their hearts are those who walk most in the fear of God. When I see a Christian living in the fear of God throughout his whole life, I know he will have much of the comfort of the Holy Spirit. It can be a means to convince others of the excellency of the ways of God. The text says that when people saw Christians walking in the fear of God, they *were multiplied*. Many were convinced by it and joined with them because they saw a beauty and excellency in their way: walking in the fear of God and in the joy of the Holy Spirit.

And this was at a time of peace and safety. Many people will seem to walk in the fear of God when they are in danger, but the early church walked with Him in a time of freedom and safety, and even then the joy of the Holy Spirit was greatly increased among them.

I will close after mentioning two or three more things:

Walking above the World
The saints walk in a way that is on high. They walk above the

world and keep themselves aloft in a spiritual way. It is true that their hearts are humble before God, yet they are lifted above the world. They consider themselves unworthy of the smallest crumb, but they see themselves as too good to be enslaved to sin or satisfied with the things of the world. Their hearts are lifted up on high to converse with the Most High God, so they are delivered from the snares of death that are below.

Walking as Christ Walked
True walkers with God endeavor to walk as Christ walked: *He that saith he abideth in him ought himself also so to walk, even as he walked* (1 John 2:6). No one ever walked with God the way Jesus Christ walked with God. No one ever had the fellowship with the Father that the Son had. Christ walked in constant fellowship with the Father. So the saints labor to walk as Christ walked, to make Him the pattern of their lives.

And so, as Christ was anointed with the oil of joy and gladness, His people have some of the ointment run down on them, and they share in the communion that Jesus Christ had with the Father by walking with Him. May the Lord bring you into this walk and keep you there.

Having seen the evidences of those who truly walk with God, we must turn to the rules of direction that guide and preserve this walk.

Chapter 8

Twelve Rules for Walking with God

You ask, "What rules should be observed for a Christian's walk with God?" I have shown you that it is a most blessed thing to walk with Him, and you are convinced of it. But what directions can be given for such a walk?

1. Guard against Every Known Sin

Be certain that no way of sin remains in you. Take heed of giving way to any sin – especially known sin, even if it seems small or is a sin of omission. To allow any known sin will make the presence of God fearful rather than sweet and will make all your duties empty rather than fruitful. It estranges God from your soul more than you realize.

You cannot have communion with God while you persist in any way of sin, especially sins against light. Even the smallest sin that a Christian gives way to is like a thorn in the foot, but a great sin against knowledge is like a great gash. If a man has a small thorn in his foot or a small piece of gravel in his shoe, he may take a step or two, but he will have to stop. Small sins are like gravel in the shoe or like a thorn in the foot.

But a greater sin – one against conscience and light – is like a deep gash cut by an axe. With such a wound, you will not be able to walk at all with comfort. With the same kind of sin wound, you need to go to the Physician of souls for healing. You need salve applied to heal your soul. Beware of sin – both the small and the great. They will hinder and cripple your walk with God.

2. Keep Your Heart Free from Earthly Entanglements

Work to detach your heart from earthly and sensual things as much as you can so that you may be spiritual. A heart weighed down with things of the world cannot walk freely with God. God is a Spirit, and you must be spiritual in your fellowship with Him.

You may use the comforts of this life, but take care not to let your heart close around them as if they are enough. Use the earthly comforts in a spiritual way, but do not defile your heart with them. Do not let them ensnare you. A man cannot walk if he is caught in a snare. When people fetter themselves in the world and entangle themselves with excessive busyness or creature contentment, it hinders their freedom in walking with God. When their hearts sink down to the creature, they cannot walk with God, for God is above. He is on high, and the way of the wise is on high, so we must keep ourselves on high.

Sometimes Christians have good affections, and their hearts are stirred up to things that are good. But at other times, their hearts sink down to the world, to sensual and earthly contentment, and they are unable to walk freely with God. At best, they can limp along like one whose legs are uneven. So when our affections are up and down – sometimes stirred up to heaven and sometimes down to the world – our walk will be haltingly weak. This up and down may even happen at the same time if some truths heave us upward, but we have a drossy spirit that pulls us back down again.

We must keep our affections even. They must not be for heaven and earth together, unless one is in subordination to the other. While we are living on earth, we can keep our hearts in heaven by keeping them in subordination to spiritual things – even when we are busied about the earthly. Then a man's heart is spiritual and separated from the earth when he knows how to have comfort in God alone, when he knows how to make up the lack of all creature comforts in God Himself.

> No Christian can walk with God unless he rests fully in Him.

How will we know if a heart is spiritual? It is spiritual when it knows how to satisfy itself in God alone and to make up the want of all creature comforts in Him. No Christian can walk with God unless he rests fully in Him, makes up everything he needs in God, and uses everything in order unto God.

3. Always Take Christ with You

If you desire to walk with God, you must always take Christ with you. God and the soul cannot walk together except through Christ the Mediator. By this I mean, in all your fellowship with God, keep your eye on Christ. Look to God, the infinite, glorious First Being of all things, but always through Christ the Mediator.

It is Christ who makes God lovely, gracious, and familiar to us. God is even a friend that the soul can have familiarity with when He is looked on through Jesus Christ. Act in Christ's strength and offer your service through Him. Those who are not acquainted with the mystery of the gospel in Christ can know little of this walk with God.

But you might say, "Enoch did not know much of Christ."

But I tell you he did. Though it was long before Christ came, Enoch's eye was on Christ. The author of Hebrews wrote: *By faith Enoch was translated that he should not see death* (Hebrews 11:5). It was all by faith. Now Christ is the object of faith, so his eye was certainly on Christ.

It was through faith, and I will give you one passage that will show the use of keeping your eye on Christ in walking with God. In Exodus 25:21-22, God told Moses: *Thou shalt put the mercy seat above upon the ark; and in the ark thou shalt put the testimony that I shall give thee. And there I will meet with thee, and I will commune with thee from above the mercy seat.* They were to meet at the mercy seat. Come to the ark, look up to the mercy seat, and I will meet with you and commune with you there.

Now what mercy seat do we have other than Jesus Christ? We must look upon God in Christ. When we do, God is rendered amiable, sweet, glorious, and lovely to us in His Son. It is there that God meets with and communes with His saints.

Apart from Christ, God appears only as a consuming fire, and we cannot expect to draw near to commune with Him. Those who look upon God merely in a legal way, look upon Him as a Judge who requires exact services and duties of them. If they cannot perform those exacting duties, they are unable to meet with and commune with God. But those who look up to the Mercy Seat look up to Christ by faith when they have to deal with God in Christ.

Oh, these people meet with God; they commune with God. There is sweet communion between God and their souls. They walk with God because, through Christ, He becomes gracious, lovely, sweet, amiable, and familiar to them.

4. Guard Your Spirit and Beautify Your Soul

Be especially careful of your spirit. God is a Spirit, and He is worshiped in spirit and in truth. When you walk with Him, your soul matters more than your outward actions. So if you want to walk with God, be very careful of your spirit. Keep your heart with all diligence, for it is with your soul that God converses. In fact, the proper sphere of a Christian is to be busy about his heart, to be busy in the inward man.

It is not so much about the outward man. If the heart is kept in a right frame, the outward man will be brought over of its own accord. But be careful of your spirit, the thoughts of your mind. Do not admit any uncleanness in your thoughts, for the soul converses with God in thoughts as well as we converse with men in words. We commune and converse with men by speech, so God gave speech to men so that they may converse with one another. What speech is to men, the thoughts are to God. We converse mostly with God by our thoughts, so labor to keep them honest and pure.

> You who call yourselves Christians, God calls you every day to walk with Him.

Guard also the affections and the stirrings of your heart, for God and your soul converse together in the workings and stirrings of your heart. Strive to adorn your soul with what will make you amiable and lovely in the eyes of God. Then the Lord will delight to converse with you and walk with you.

If you were called out to walk with a superior, with some nobleman, you would dress for the occasion. So you must clothe your soul with graces when called to walk with God. You who call yourselves Christians, God calls you every day to walk with Him. And if you expect to have communion with Him and God to delight in you, you must labor to beautify your souls. Dress yourself with those things that may make you amiable in the eyes of God and do not come into the presence of God filthy and unclean.

What is it that makes the soul amiable in the eyes of God? Holiness. It is the very image of God, and He delights to walk with one where He can see His own image. The more resplendent the image of God is in the soul, the more the Lord delights to walk with such a soul.

Labor for the behavior of your soul to be suitable to God. When I walk with a superior, I need to have a demeanor that is suitable for his presence. As it was said before, to walk with God is to walk in the fear of God. Be aware of your spirit. Beautify your soul in what makes you lovely in God's eyes and carry yourself as is fitting for His presence.

I will only mention one passage about the beautifying of the soul. Psalm 45 describes the church and the saints being brought in to the presence of God: *The king's daughter is all glorious within: her clothing is of wrought gold* (Psalm 45:13). Many make a great show of things on the outside, but the king's daughter, the church, is all glorious within. The next verse states: *She shall be brought unto the king in raiment of needlework.* She will be brought to the King, to Jesus Christ, with garments of needlework – the many graces of the Spirit of God that puts beauty on the soul. The varied graces of the Spirit are her ornament, like the beauty of needlework. So let your soul be clothed with holiness, for God delights to walk with someone who is lovely in His eyes.

5. Avoid Halting between Two Ways

When you walk with God, you must not go back and forth but must give yourself fully to Him. Do not have a distracted heart or a divided heart between two opinions: *How long halt ye between two opinions? if the* LORD *be God, follow him: but if*

Baal, then follow him (1 Kings 18:21). A distracted or divided heart, one not resolved in the way of God, cannot walk steadily.

When the soul is truly resolved, it says, "If I cannot be happy here, I am content to be miserable here; for I know this is the only path where true happiness can be found. Whatever appearances to the contrary flesh and blood may raise, I know there is enough here to bless my soul forever. So whatever comes, I am determined to walk in these ways."

That is the soul that is fit to walk with God. It does not halt but takes straight steps in the ways of God. The author of Hebrews requires this of us: *Make straight paths for your feet, lest that which is lame be turned out of the way* (Hebrews 12:13). To walk straight means to follow God's way without longing after something else.

Many have convictions of conscience that incline their hearts toward God's paths, and they even begin to walk in them – yet their hearts are drawn to the world. When the heart truly walks with God, it gives up itself wholly to Him, without division, and is resolved to go on.

Some may start well with good thoughts and intentions, but if their hearts are divided between God and the world, they will eventually turn aside and become apostates. That which is lame will be turned out of the way; the ways of God will be tedious to you when you do not give up yourselves wholly to them. This is why so many fall away. They seemed to go in God's ways but only haltingly. His ways grew tedious, and in the end, they turned aside.

6. Beware of Formality in Holy Duties

Take heed of mere formality when you come to holy duties. Labor to stir up your heart and press for the power of godliness in them. You must strive to get up to God in them. It is a good thing to keep close to the duty in our performance of them, but that is not enough – you must keep close to God in the duty. We must work to not only stay focused on the duty but also keep close to God, to find God in all the duties we perform. Take pains to find God in all the ordinances. Do not rest satisfied or quiet your heart until you find God.

God Himself said something about this: *In all places where I record my name I will come unto thee, and I will bless thee* (Exodus 20:24). Wherever there is any ordinance or any holy duty to be performed, there is a recording of God's name. And He said He would come there and bless you. If you want to walk with God, you must go where God is and be in those places where He comes.

God walks in His ordinances and in His worship; therefore, you must be very spiritual in worship and sanctify the name of God there. You must urge your hearts and all that is within you to walk with God there and not be satisfied until you have something of God.

Bernard said something remarkable: "I never go from thee without thee." Whenever we pray, worship, or participate in the ordinances, we must not be satisfied until we meet God there and leave carrying something of God with us.

7. Guard against Quiet Drifting

Be careful of drifting away from God's ways in subtle, almost unnoticeable steps. You who profess your desire to walk with God will not in an open way forsake God and His ways, but if you are not very watchful over your hearts, they will quietly wander away from the ways of God, from those paths where you used to have communion with Him. Be careful not to turn from God's paths. Temptations, especially those that match your weaknesses, will promise ease and contentment to your flesh and can lure you from the paths of God.

Peter warned of false teachers who lured people through fleshly desires: *When they speak great swelling words of vanity, they allure through the lusts of the flesh, through much wantonness, those that were clean escaped from them who live in error* (2 Peter 2:18). There were some who had escaped from sinful, ungodly ways. They were not hypocrites. They really had escaped and were not just making a show of right living. But they had broken free of those sins – not by the Spirit's saving power, but by the light of their conscience. So they were especially susceptible to being tempted away through the lusts of the flesh, through wantonness, by those who taught false doctrine. They are easy prey for teaching that seems to offer both godliness and freedom for the flesh.

> May the Lord deliver young beginners from the wantons of our age.

Oh, beware. Some have been walking with God but then met with these people who offer this tempting but false teaching. You can tell it is false if it gives liberty to the flesh, but these people think it offers a fine, even, and smooth way. They see a path that lets them have both devotion to God and indulgence of their desires.

But it is different for those who have been changed by God. There is no way to lure those who have escaped from the ways of sin by the power of the Word. There is no way to tempt them to believe that they may make a profession of godliness and yet have liberty in the flesh too.

Oh, may the Lord deliver young beginners from the wantons of our age, from those who lure them through the lusts of the flesh and promise liberty to them. The text adds: *While they promise them liberty, they themselves are the servants of corruption* (2 Peter 2:19). Those who promise them liberty and bring such a doctrine of liberty to you are themselves the servants to sin.

Take care not to slide into the ways of the flesh after you seemed to begin in the spirit. You who seemed to converse with God and walk with Him, what evil have you now found in Him that you should leave Him? Are His ways too difficult for you? If so, your heart is still base. It has not been changed and made suitable to what is spiritual and holy.

May God's angel meet with those who are sliding away from His good and blessed ways. We read in Genesis that the angel met Hagar when she was fleeing from Abraham's family, from the church of God. He asked her: *Whence camest thou?* (Genesis 16:8). Do you come from Abraham's family? Are you really leaving there? Where are you going to find someplace better than Abraham's family where the presence of God is?

Let God meet with you who are drifting away from God. O soul, where are you going? You had the Word working on your heart, and you seemed to be turned into the good ways of God. What will be the end of the ways you are walking in now? True, they give contentment to the flesh more than former ways, but do you think the end of them will be peace?

Oh, I wish there were such a messenger from God to meet you in those ways you are walking in so that you may say as the church does in Hosea: *I will go and return to my first husband; for then was it better with me than now* (Hosea 2:7). I used to have more peace, comfort, and sweetness in conversing with God in holy duties than I find now, so I will return to those ways of God. The ways of God may be scorned and derided by many, but they are the only ways that lead to lasting peace and sweetness of soul.

8. Keep a Tender Spirit toward the First Signs of Sliding

If you have begun to wander, labor to keep a tender spirit – one that feels even the first stirrings of decline. It is true that while we are here on this earth, we have a great deal of corruption, and our hearts are drawn quickly from the ways of God. But if we are watchful and sensitive, we might still keep our walk with God. If, at the very moment we took one step away from God, we stopped and asked, "Where are we? What are we doing?" we would turn back and not drift so far from Him.

It is dangerous for people to go far from God. When they do, they begin to despair. He begins to grow desperate and plunges full force into sin, seeking to satisfy the lusts of the flesh with greediness. Some men are convinced in their consciences that they are off of the right path, but even though they know it, they go further and further from God.

Why? How is that possible? Because they once professed Christ, and now that they have departed from Him, the devil follows them with despairing thoughts. He tells them that God will not accept them if they return to Him, so they might as well fully satisfy their lusts.

I truly believe this is why so many apostates turn so notoriously wicked. When you see a man who had once been zealous in religion not only fall away, but fall far and is now a drunkard, a scoffer, or worse, you can almost be sure this is the ground of it: Though his conscience is convinced that he is out of the way, he is desperate to have his pleasure because he thinks God has forsaken him. But he has forsaken God, and he is determined to fulfill his lusts. And that is all the poor creature will have to satisfy himself with. Be careful not to get too far from God. Be tender to the first beginnings of sliding away and turn back quickly, lest hopelessness and despair harden you beyond return.

9. Be Spiritual in Solitary Time

If you want to walk with God, prize your solitary hours. Labor to be spiritual in them. Do not waste them. When you are alone – when no one but God and you are together – labor to be spiritual. Especially you who have much business in the world – you make such little use of your alone times. You do not know what to do with them. But they are excellent opportunities. Say to yourself, "Now I am apart from the world; now I can deal with God and my own soul. I will not rest, I will not be quiet until I have conversed with Him."

Christians who are spiritual when alone will be spiritual when in company. As Moses's face shone after spending time alone with God on the mountain, so Christians who are alone and spiritual with God will shine in holy conversation and conduct with others.

10. Count God's Presence Better than All the World

Let the presence of God be more to you than all the world. It should matter more to your soul that you are in the presence of God than if the whole world were watching you. The spirits of men and women would be so much more quieted and composed if they had a fearful reverence of the presence of God and valued it more than all the world; and if they would not do anything in God's presence that they would be ashamed to do before the whole world. Prize God's presence and seek His approval above all.

11. Continue in Duty Though Comfort Is Lacking

Resolve to go on in the performance of holy duties even when you see no fruit at present. Though you lack the comfort you desire, you are still in the path of obedience, and that should satisfy every gracious heart. It is better to walk in God's way without encouragement than to turn to another path. Keep in the way of God.

12. Interpret God's Dealings with You for Good

Learn to put a good interpretation on all of God's ways with you. This will greatly help you to walk steadily with Him. If He comes in affliction, do not conclude that God is your enemy. That will discourage you from keeping to God's path. Rather, see that God intends good in every trial. Believing that will help keep you walking close to Him in every condition. If God seems to go out of the way of prosperity and come in the way of affliction, make good interpretations of it. Do not think God is leaving you or forsaking you. Instead, exercise faith in this and believe that God may intend as much good to you in that way as in any other way.

> Learn to put a good interpretation on all of God's ways with you.

The writer of Hebrews reminds us that chastening is a mark of sonship. *My son, despise not thou the chastening of the Lord, nor faint when thou art rebuked of him: for whom the Lord loveth he chasteneth, and scourgeth every son whom he receiveth. If ye endure chastening, God dealeth with you as with sons; for what son is he whom the father chasteneth not? But if ye be without chastisement, whereof all are partakers, then are ye bastards, and not sons* (Hebrews 12:5-8). If you endure chastisements, God deals with you as a father with his child.

The writer speaks more of chastisements in verses 9-11, and then he draws a conclusion, based on the fact that we are to look on God as a father in His chastisements: *Wherefore lift up the hands which hang down, and the feeble knees; and make straight paths for your feet, lest that which is lame be turned out of the way* (Hebrews 12:12-13). When you apprehend God in a way of wrath against you and not in a way of love, your knees will be feeble, and you will not be able to go on with that cheerfulness and to walk with God in that hard way that He seems to call you to.

But if you look on yourselves as sons, and you understand that God intends good for you, then by chastisements, you may be made partakers of His holiness. He tells you to lift up your hands that hang down and those feeble knees – those feeble knees that were so weak you were unable to walk with God. Those feeble knees will be strengthened if you make good interpretation of the ways of God and believe that the Lord intends good to you.

And when outward afflictions are joined with inward trials – when God comes against your soul with spiritual afflictions, you must interpret them rightly as well.

You might argue that those times are the hardest to walk with God. It is true. We may walk with and keep in communion with God during outward afflictions, but when the Lord seems to withdraw Himself and when there are both outward and inward trials, that is hard.

One notable example of a child of God following hard after Him though He seemed to withdraw Himself from the soul was David. From the title of Psalm 63, we find that David was in the wilderness of Judah, and Saul was chasing him to take his life. Saul persecuted and followed David, forcing him to flee from place to place. Yet he said, *O God, thou art my God; early will I seek thee: my soul thirsteth for thee, my flesh longeth for thee in a dry and thirsty land, where no water is. . . . My soul followeth hard after thee* (Psalm 63:1; 8). Though You, Lord, seem to have withdrawn Yourself from me in regard to these outward trials, my soul follows hard after You.

If in times of affliction, when God seems to withdraw

Himself, when it seems He does not want to walk with us – oh, run after Him! If a mother gets ahead of her child and he loses sight of her, the child cries out and runs after her. David did the same thing. When it seemed that God was going away from him, he said that his soul followed hard after Him. The spirit is in good condition when, instead of giving up or growing cold when God feels absent, it follows harder after God. Nothing can satisfy it but God Himself.

David said that in a dry land his soul thirsted – not for water, but for God. So, in affliction, say with David, "Lord, it is not mere deliverance from suffering that I seek, but You. If I can have more of You in this time of trial, that is enough for me."

Chapter 9

When God Seems to Hide His Face: An Objection Answered

If the Lord seems to withdraw Himself from the spirits of His servants, what guidance can be given for walking with God in such a time of spiritual desertion? You may say, "You have told us of the excellency of walking with God, and we count it the happiness of our lives to walk with Him. But God will not walk with me – He withdraws Himself from my soul. I cannot see Him, for He hides His face from me." To such as feel that God has withdrawn, I have several things to say.

Be Comforted

Be of good comfort. It is a good sign that God has made you know what it is to walk with Him since you can feel His withdrawing. There is a generation of people in the world who walk lightly in the profession of religion, and they never notice God's absence. They never complain of any such thing because they do not know what it means – they have never known His presence. But if you are sensible of His leaving, it shows you have known something of God's walking with you.

Examine Yourself

Examine whether you have sometimes shut God out when He offered to walk with you. Has God not tendered Himself, even taken you by the hand, yet you were not at leisure then, and your mind was occupied elsewhere? Oh! Be humbled before Him for all your unworthy dealings with Him and for all your wandering from Him. Know that God calls you to this, but your spirit has wandered from God many times.

Say with David of your spiritual wanderings as he said of his: *Thou tellest my wanderings: put thou my tears into thy bottle: are they not in thy book?* (Psalm 56:8). "Lord, my spirit has wandered many times but put my tears in Your bottle. Let my tears match my wanderings. It grieves me to the soul that I have ever grieved Your Spirit. When Your Spirit has tried to take me by the hand, I have pulled away and grieved Him. Oh, it grieves my soul! Oh Lord, You have noticed my wanderings. Take notice of my genuine tears."

Affliction Is Better than Sin

It is better for God to withdraw than for us to withdraw. If God withdraws from you, it is your affliction; but if you withdraw from God, it is your sin – and sin is far worse than affliction. It is better to endure any affliction, even sharp spiritual affliction, than to commit sin.

You who complain that God has withdrawn and will not walk with you – remember, your own withdrawing is a greater evil to you than His. It is true, God withdrawing from me is the most painful affliction I have ever known in this world; but my withdrawing from Him is a greater burden to me.

And it may be that if God had not withdrawn from you, you would have withdrawn from Him. Many times, God withdrew from His people to prevent His people from withdrawing from Him. As a mother may hide herself from her child so that the child does not wander, so God sometimes hides Himself because He sees your heart growing careless, wanton, or vain. By withdrawing, He stirs you to cling more closely and follow after Him more earnestly.

But take heed: If God withdraws and you do not cry after Him, or if you grow weary and stop crying, then you are in true danger. It is like a child who has lost his mother or father. At first, he cries, but then a beggar comes and entices him with an apple or plum and steals the child away. The child is quieted for the moment but to his ruin. Therefore, hold fast. Do not depart from the Lord. Keep crying after Him, even in His withdrawing.

Absence of Comfort Is Not Absence of God

Remember this: God's withdrawing of comfort is not always the withdrawing of His presence. You may mistakenly think that God has withdrawn because He has taken away your comfort, but that may be a great mistake.

This is a sure rule – use it often when your comforts are gone: God may withdraw comfort without withdrawing His presence. He may still be with you in His grace and support. As David said: *My soul followeth hard after thee: thy right hand upholdeth me* (Psalm 63:8). Though God seemed absent, His hand upheld him. In the same way, God may be present to uphold and strengthen you and to exercise your faith in Him. That may be as acceptable to God as when you walked in the fullness of comfort. The exercise of faith in the absence of comfort may contain as much of God as all the comforts you ever had in all your life. Therefore, do not say that God's presence is gone merely because your comforts are gone.

> **Do not say that God's presence is gone merely because your comforts are gone.**

Think of the sun. In winter it shines brightly, but its beams are not so effectual as the hidden influence of the sun in summer when it is behind a cloud. Is the presence of the sun gone in the summer simply because there is a cloud between the sun and you? A child may think so, but we know better. We can feel its influence – the warmth of the day and the light that allows us to work – though it does not shine as directly as before. Meanwhile, the bright winter sun, for all its shining, does not bring the same power to make the plants grow.

So it is with God's presence. At times, the beams of His presence may seem clouded to a Christian by outward afflictions, yet there may be more of God in such a time than when you bask in the brightness of comfort. The shining of the comforts of a Christian may be compared to the shining of the sun in the winter – it gives light but sometimes has no influence to sanctify the heart, just as the winter sun cannot bring forth fruit. But when the sun is hidden in another season, it still gives life to the earth. In the same way, though God may withhold the shining of outward comforts, He may shine on your soul, increase His grace in you, and make you more fruitful than ever before.

Even If You Do Not See His Face, Hear His Voice

If you cannot see God's face, then listen for His voice and follow it. Perhaps in private prayer you cannot see His face as you once did. But when you come to the Word, do you not hear His voice? God is pleased to speak to your soul through His Word, so thank Him and follow His voice, even if it is in the dark. As the voice of a parent comforts a crying, lost child, so the voice of God comforts those who cannot see His face. They may not receive the same comforts from God they have had in the past – the sweet manifestations of His love shed abroad in their hearts (Romans 5:5). But when they read the Word, they cannot help but say they hear their Father's voice.

Perhaps the Word is not as comforting to you as it was in the past, but is it not still a directing Word, an instructing Word, an enlightening Word? That is enough to sustain you for the present time.

Wait in His Ways

The last thing I will say is this: Keep yourself in a waiting frame for God. Do not conclude that because the Lord is gone, He will be gone forever. Remain in the ways of God, waiting for Him. Resolve that though God may withdraw, you will not leave the path where you once found Him. If you are sure God was once there, then stay on that path where you used to meet with Him, and you will meet with Him again.

It is better to keep to the ordinary highway of God, for you are far more likely to meet with Him there than if you wander elsewhere. I will conclude with a Scripture or two. The first is in Psalm 101:2: *I will behave myself wisely in a perfect way. O when wilt thou come unto me?* I cite this verse because of the way David resolved to walk wisely and uprightly, even while longing for God's presence: "Lord, You are absent from me now, but I will not leave the way in which I used to find You. Oh, when will You come?" He did not despair of ever seeing God again, but he hoped that he would afterward.

> Keep yourself in a waiting frame for God.

The second passage is also from Psalms: *I will keep thy statutes: O forsake me not utterly* (Psalm 119:8). It seemed to David, in his present sense, that the Lord had forsaken him. But what was David's resolution? Did he say, "God has forsaken me, and I will forsake Him"? No. He said, "I will keep Your statutes; do not leave me utterly!"

So, keep on in the ways of God still. Walk in His paths and wait for His presence until He comes – and conclude this: Surely, He will come.

Do not be like children who, when they see the sun go down, think it has vanished forever and will never rise again. Though God seems to withdraw the light of His face from you, do not conclude that you will never again enjoy His comforts in communion with Him. Do not say that. Go on, keep in the ways of God. Wait on Him and look up toward Him so you may once more know as much communion, sweetness, and joy in God as you have ever known in your life.

And know this: God calls for the work of faith in such times as these. Now He calls you to walk by faith and not by sight.

About the Author

Jeremiah Burroughs, born in 1599 in East Anglia, England, was a prominent English Puritan preacher known for his love for the Lord and for his deep theological insight. Though specific details of his early family life remain unclear, records show that he was baptized in 1601 and entered Emmanuel College, Cambridge, in 1617. There he came under the influence of Puritan leaders like Thomas Hooker. He earned a B.A. in 1621 and an M.A. in 1624 but left the university because of his refusal to conform to certain practices of the Church of England.

Shortly after his time at Cambridge, Burroughs began ministerial work in Suffolk under Edmund Calamy the Elder at Bury St Edmunds. Both men became known for their refusal to read the *Book of Sports*, a royal proclamation that permitted recreational activities on Sundays, which many Puritans believed profaned the Sabbath. This stance marked Burroughs early on as a committed nonconformist. In 1631, he became rector of Tivetshall in Norfolk, where he ministered faithfully until 1636 or 1637, when he was suspended and eventually removed from his post by Bishop Matthew Wren. His offenses included refusing to bow at the mention of the name of Jesus during church services, declining to use prescribed prayers, and continuing to preach extemporaneously.

After his dismissal, Burroughs went into exile in the Netherlands, joining an English-speaking Independent (Congregationalist) congregation in Rotterdam. There he served alongside other influential Puritans, including William Bridge and Sidrach Simpson. His time abroad solidified his convictions about church governance and religious liberty, and he became a strong advocate for the autonomy of local congregations.

With the outbreak of the English Civil War, Burroughs returned to England in 1641 and became pastor of two congregations in London – Stepney and St Giles Cripplegate. His morning sermons in Stepney earned him the affectionate title "the morning star of Stepney." His preaching was marked by clarity, doctrinal richness, and pastoral warmth. He became highly respected among his peers, and Thomas Brooks would later call him "a prince of preachers." He was also invited to preach before both Houses of Parliament, a significant honor for any minister of his time.

Burroughs was chosen in 1643 as a member of the Westminster Assembly, a body tasked with reforming the Church of England. There, he aligned with a group of ministers known as the "Dissenting Brethren," who favored Congregationalist church polity over the more centralized Presbyterian model. Along with Thomas Goodwin, William Bridge, Philip Nye, and Sidrach Simpson, he signed the *Apologeticall Narration* in 1644, a document that defended the legitimacy of independent churches while also appealing for unity with fellow believers. Although deeply committed to his theological positions, Burroughs was remarkably irenic in his manner. He displayed this spirit of peace in the motto posted above the door to his study: "Opinionum varietas et opinantium unitas non sunt ασυστατα" – "Variety of opinion and unity of believers are not incompatible."

About the Author

Even Richard Baxter, who often clashed with Independents, praised Burroughs for his gentleness and conciliatory nature. Baxter famously stated, "If all the Episcopalians had been like Archbishop Ussher, all the Presbyterians like Stephen Marshall, and all the Independents like Jeremiah Burroughs, the breaches of the church would soon have been healed." Burroughs' legacy is thus one of peacemaking as well as preaching.

Many of Burroughs works were published posthumously. His most well-known book is *The Rare Jewel of Christian Contentment*, which continues to be widely read today. Other important titles include *Gospel Worship*, *Gospel Fear*, *The Evil of Evils*, *Hope*, and *The Excellency of a Gracious Spirit*. These writings display his pastoral concern for the spiritual well-being of believers and his deep love for the gospel of Christ. His exposition of Hosea, spanning multiple volumes, reflects his dedication to thorough biblical teaching.

Burroughs died in November 1646 at the age of 47, following injuries sustained from a fall from his horse after returning from a session of the Westminster Assembly. His death was mourned widely in London and among Puritans across England. Though his life was cut short, his influence endured through his writings and through the example he left of a preacher who combined doctrinal firmness with humility and peace.

For those reading his books today, Burroughs offers a refreshing blend of theological depth and godly wisdom. He speaks especially to Christians seeking to live with joyful contentment and spiritual maturity. His life and legacy continue to inspire those pursuing truth and grace in the Lord Jesus Christ.

Also by Jeremiah Burroughs

Gospel Worship
by Jeremiah Burroughs

In this piercing yet refreshing series of sermons, the beloved Puritan preacher Jeremiah Burroughs calls believers to a reverent, Scripture-based approach to worship. Originally delivered during the 1600s, preserved from his pulpit notes and now in updated, modern English, *Gospel Worship* is a sobering reminder that drawing near to God is no frivolous matter. How we worship reveals what we believe about the God we worship.

With careful exposition of Leviticus 10:3, Burroughs shows that worship must be governed by God's Word, not our inventions. He exposes the subtle dangers of "strange fire" (practices which God has not commanded) and pleads with readers to truly reverence the Lord in the ordinances: in prayer, in hearing the Word, and in the Lord's Supper

Profound, practical, and deeply convicting, *Gospel Worship* is both a theological treatise and a devotional aid – meant to reform our worship and rekindle our reverence for our awesome and powerful God.

Available where books are sold and free as an eBook

www.ingramcontent.com/pod-product-compliance
Lightning Source LLC
LaVergne TN
LVHW010325070526
838199LV00065B/5652